THE ANTS' GOLD

by the same author

ZANSKAR: THE HIDDEN KINGDOM
THE GREAT HIMALAYAN PASSAGE
THE CAVALIERS OF KHAM:THE SECRET WAR IN TIBET
LORDS AND LAMAS
MUSTANG: A LOST TIBETAN KINGDOM
TIGER FOR BREAKFAST
THE LOST WORLD OF QUINTANA-ROO

THE ANTS' GOLD

The Discovery of the Greek El Dorado in the Himalayas

MICHEL PEISSEL

HARVILL PRESS
8 Grafton Street, London W1
1984

To Missy

Harvill Press Ltd
is distributed by
William Collins Sons and Co. Ltd
London · Glasgow · Sydney · Auckland
Toronto · Johannesburg

British Library Cataloguing in Publication Data

Peissel, Michel
The ants' gold.
1. Himalaya Mountain—Description and travel
I. Title
915.4'0452   DS485.H6

ISBN 0 00 272514 2

First published in 1984 by Harvill Press Ltd
© Michel Peissel, 1984

Printed in Great Britain

ACKNOWLEDGEMENTS

I wish here to express my thanks to and admiration for Sheikh Abdullah, the Lion of Kashmir, the late Chief Minister of the State of Jammu and Kashmir; a man whose eminence and old age did not impede him from giving me, over the years, valuable counsel and assistance on my quests. In his memory I broke the laws of India, in the hope that perhaps some day less enlightened politicians might learn the importance of those endeavours that concern our most valuable heritage, our past.

I wish to thank Mr Ghulam Muhammed Kakpori for kindly sharing with us his enlightened research on the Drok-pa of Ladakh, and to ask his forgiveness for having deceived him.

In particular I want to thank Sonam and Tashi, two men from Dartzig, whom I also had to mislead in order to complete our mission.

Lastly I wish to thank Nordrop Lama, whose enthusiasm kept us going over the most arduous mountain trails.

CONTENTS

List of illustrations   *page ix*

 1 Dreams and Reality   1
 2 Cease-fire   10
 3 Human Sacrifice   22
 4 A Stone Age Artist   38
 5 The Kingdom of Women   52
 6 The Gold of the Indus   63
 7 The Unicorn and the Fairies   77
 8 Poisoned Arrows   91
 9 Operation Ibex   110
10 The Death of the Lion   122
11 The Gold-Digging Ants   134
12 In Disguise   150
13 The Lost Horizon   161

   Postscript   175
   Index   177

ILLUSTRATIONS

between pages 52 and 53

Missy Allen at the camp above Gyagam
Lama Nordrop
Ancient carving of an ibex-hunting scene
Minaro drawing of hunting with a crossbow
The author
Donjé Nacugya with the village chief of Thunri
A Minaro girl
An old Minaro man
Missy with Sonam and Tashi
Marmots on the plain of Dansar

Unless otherwise specified, all photographs are from the collection of the author.

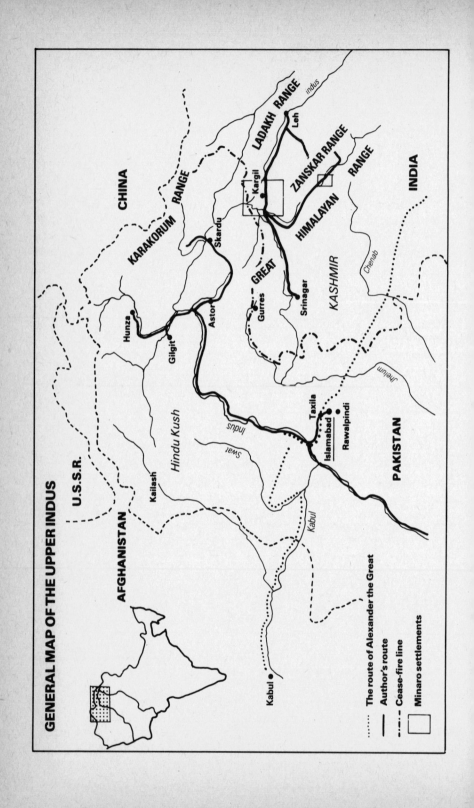

GENERAL MAP OF THE UPPER INDUS

U.S.S.R.

AFGHANISTAN

CHINA

KARAKORUM RANGE

LADAKH RANGE

ZANSKAR RANGE

HIMALAYAN RANGE

INDIA

Kailash

Hindu Kush

Hunza

Gilgit

Astor

Skardu

Indus

Swat

Kabul

Kabul

Taxila

Islamabad

Rawalpindi

PAKISTAN

Kargil

Leh

Indus

GREAT

Gurres

Srinagar

KASHMIR

Chenab

Jhelum

.... The route of Alexander the Great
——— Author's route
–·–·– Cease-fire line
▢ Minaro settlements

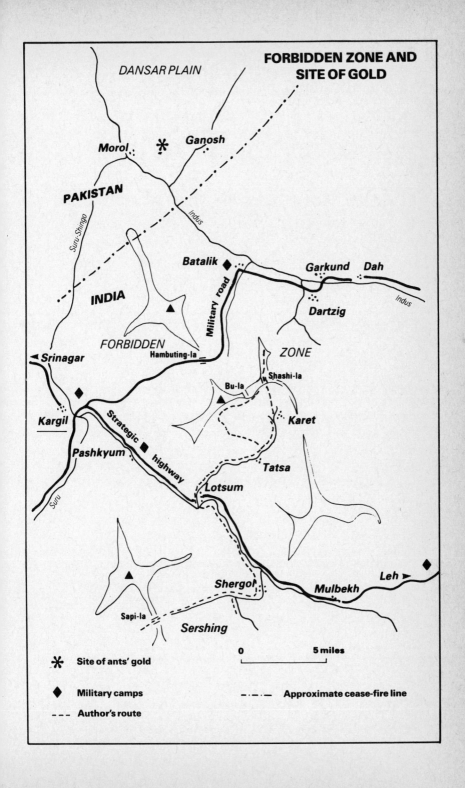

FORBIDDEN ZONE AND SITE OF GOLD

DANSAR PLAIN

Morol ✳ *Ganosh*

PAKISTAN

Suru-Shingo

Indus

INDIA

Batalik ◆

Garkund Dah

Military road

Indus

Dartzig

FORBIDDEN

◄ Srinagar

Hambuting-la

ZONE

Shashi-la

Bu-la ▲

Karet

◆

Kargil

Pashkyum ◆

Strategic *highway*

Tatsa

Lotsum

Suru

▲

◆

Leh ►

Shergol

Mulbekh

Sapi-la

Sershing

✳ Site of ants' gold

0   5 miles

◆ Military camps

–·–·– Approximate cease-fire line

- - - Author's route

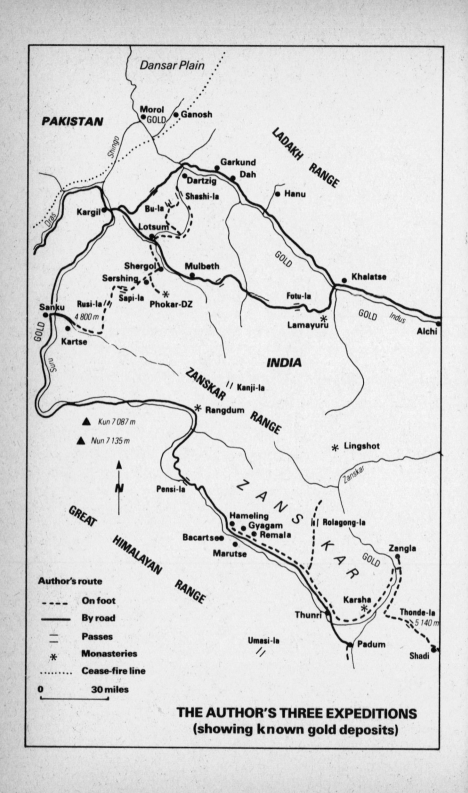

THE AUTHOR'S THREE EXPEDITIONS
(showing known gold deposits)

I

DREAMS AND REALITY

It was seven o'clock on a cold September night when three men filed past the police post at Lotsum. In the dark they must have appeared to be farmers returning late to the shelter of their homes. Three men in rags, who walked in a slouching gait. One of them was stooped, his hands beside his face holding a head strap that ran over his dirty woollen cap to the small bag on his back.

I was the tallest of the three men. I had darkened my skin with walnut juice and dyed my hair so as to pass unnoticed, with my two companions, into the forbidden border zone along the volatile Indo-Pakistan cease-fire line in the heart of the Himalayas.

Perhaps more surprising than my disguise was the nature of my mission. I was looking for gold, gold mined by ants larger than foxes!

To understand what I was doing it is necessary to start far, far back – in fact at the very beginning of our written history, in 450 BC. It was then that Herodotus, earliest of the Greek historian-geographers, wrote his famous Histories, for which he became known not only as the Father of History but also by the less flattering title of Father of Liars. His book abounded with unbeliev-able tales, of flying snakes who ate their partners and whose entrails were eaten out by their own children; of people with only one eye; of trees which grew wool as fine as that of any sheep. Of all these tales none struck the imagination more than Herodotus' story of 'gold-digging ants', ants larger than foxes yet smaller than dogs which dug up astonishing amounts of gold-bearing sand in a land located somewhere north of India.

Over the centuries the ant story travelled far and wide, cropping up in Chinese, Indian and Mongolian literature as well as in Tibetan historical documents. It was recounted by Megasthenes, recorded by the Greek geographer Strabo (who thought Herodotus a fool), told again by Arrian, Dio Chrysostom and many other Greek authors. Associated with the story was the name of a mysterious people who were believed to have collected the gold, the Dardicae or Dards. By the time the legend reached the ears of the Romans, Pliny the Elder, in his *Natural History*, exclaimed, '*Fertilissimi sunt auri Dardae*': 'Abundant is the gold of the Dards.' The story, repeated from person to person over the ages, was whispered around the camp fires of the troops of Alexander the Great on their way to India, where the great conqueror himself hoped to discover the ants' gold. Yet despite dozens of expeditions and centuries of searching, the ants and their gold were never found. As a result today most scholars believe that it was but a 'remarkable tall tale', or simply one more of Herodotus' lies, just another classical myth.

This is the story of my own long and circuitous quest for the ants' gold: a quest that took me all over the Himalayas in search of clues to Tibet's ancient past, a search which ultimately led me in disguise into a strange land set in the most inaccessible fold deep within the mountains.

From the very beginning it promised to be an unusual expedition. Although it is difficult to say when an expedition actually starts, this journey began taking shape when I flew to Boston in the spring of 1979. The Boston to New York shuttle is hardly an exciting flight, yet my heart raced at the announcement of our landing. To me it was like looping the loop, for it had been just twenty years since I had left the Harvard Business School and flown out of Boston on my first expedition to the Himalayas.

Twenty years, and what a loop it had been. I had turned my back on the prospects of a career as a businessman and had chosen adventure in favour of security. Adventures I had certainly had, but now it was, I feared, time for a sobering reappraisal.

Could there really be anything left to explore, I wondered, now that spy satellites circled a globe mapped to within inches, paced by geologists and combed by prospectors when not simply overrun by tourists? Perhaps, as some of my friends had suggested, it was time that I settled down or, as others less politely put it, grew up. The fact was that against all probability I had been able, in the twentieth century, to live out my childhood dreams. For twenty years I had roamed the Himalayas in quest of lost horizons and had been lucky enough to encounter some truly unexplored lands. Surely, like all dreams, this would come to an end. Yet here I was, still dreaming of adventure, returning to Harvard to comb its libraries for information about a mysterious people I had encountered a few years previously in the heart of the western Himalayas.

I had first seen them in the village of Mulbekh, situated half-way along the ancient trade route which links Kashmir with Tibet. It was an area inhabited by slant-eyed, Tibetan-speaking people of Mongolian appearance, so it came to me as a shock to bump into a small crowd of fair-skinned, long-nosed individuals who looked like Europeans. The men wore large bouquets of fresh flowers on their heads which gave them the look of ageing Western hippies; the women were startlingly beautiful, with fair skin, pale eyes, thin noses and numerous long braids of fine hair. Who were they? I wanted to know. The information I managed to glean was strangely conflicting. Some people told me that they were descendants of the troops of Alexander the Great, others that they were pure Aryans and that their villages along the upper Indus constituted the cradle of Aryanism, whatever that meant. When I inquired as to their name I was told they were called Drok-pa. In Tibetan Drok-pa simply means herder, a name generally given to the Mongolian-featured nomads of Tibet.

I was puzzled that these European-looking people of the Ladakh region of Kashmir should bear the same name as Tibetan nomads when they were so evidently different physically. Strange stories circulated about the Ladakhi Drok-pa. They were declared to be the dirtiest people in the world, and this by the Tibetans who themselves hardly washed at all. One rumour was that beautiful young German women had set out to have children by the Drok-pa in order to 'improve the Master Race' on Hitler's orders. Intrigued by this, I wanted to go to their villages and immediately find out more, but I discovered to my disappointment that the three valleys in which most of the 800 surviving Drok-pa lived were forbidden to foreigners, being within the highly restricted military zone of the Indus along the Pakistani border in what is known as Little Tibet.

My most exciting discovery, however, was learning that many people, including several scholars, referred to the Ladakhi Drok-pa as Dards, the very name Herodotus and other Greek writers had used to identify the inhabitants of the region of the gold-digging ants.

At first I was less interested in the ants' gold than in identifying who the Drok-pa might really be. My interest in prehistory had led me over the years to speculate that in the secluded valleys of the world's highest land mass there might still live people who could be the missing link with our own ancient past. For I knew that in the Himalayas many strange traditions survived, mementoes of a world that elsewhere had long vanished. It was in the vague hope of solving some of these mysteries of our past that I had come back to Harvard, quite unaware as to where such a quest would eventually lead me.

With nostalgia I crossed once again the old bridge which links the Harvard Business School with the rest of the university. I headed first for the Peabody Museum, whose musty odour of mouldering totem poles and rotting balsa canoes had always seemed to me to be that of a true antechamber to adventure. I found the museum empty. Most of the professors I had known were dead. As for my classmates from the Business School, they were now far away swinging on the upper rungs of corporate ladders. What had I achieved, I asked myself, after twenty years spent chasing childhood fantasies? I had acquired neither fame nor fortune; at best a string of vivid memories of remote passes and lonely monasteries, and a year-round suntan. Some claimed I had even acquired an Oriental air in spite of my long nose. I felt alone in a world of memories, and again began to doubt everything, my beliefs, my aims, myself. Was I but a dreamer, I asked myself, as I wandered over to the Weidner Library to begin my research.

While at Harvard I met a tall, elegant young woman whose green eyes and long legs belied her position as Director of Admissions at the Graduate School. Very quickly I found myself cheering up as I expounded to her the beauties of the Himalayas, the rugged mountains and the mysteries they contained. Maybe it was to reassure myself that I began claiming that in spite of the satellites circling our globe, there was still much to discover, many areas of the world yet unexplored because they were either too remote or, more commonly, inaccessible for political reasons. In a paroxysm of enthusiasm I told her the remarkable tale of the gold-digging ants and the strange, hippie-like Drok-pa. 'You must understand,' I explained, 'it is in the Himalayas that our past is preserved in living form. Everywhere else the world is dying of culture shock as remote countries absorb the tenets of Western civilization. The Himalayas are different; there are still places where the West is not yet present. There are still entire regions whose science, medicine, technology, beliefs and customs remain the product of slow maturation which, from generation to generation, links man back to his earliest ancestors.'

I had reached a crescendo of fervour when I turned to my new scholarly friend and asked, 'Why don't you come with me?' To my amazement the answer was 'Sure!' Thus Missy Allen became my collaborator and companion in my search for the identity of the guardians of the ants' gold.

If exploring deep gorges and crossing high passes is a very exciting occupation I found an almost equal thrill in plunging down into the bowels of the fifteen storeys of metallic shelves of the Weidner Library – shelves connected by ancient rattling staircases, the technological entrails of some sort of think factory.

Every day for several months Missy and I moved about the library, searching for enlightenment regarding the Dards whom Herodotus had described as the 'bravest of all Indians'. Like the ants, I too burrowed for gold. I soon discovered that I was not the first to have searched for their location. Indeed, this quest had fascinated hundreds before me, among them such famous scholars as Sir Aurel Stein and B. Laufer, together with a whole assortment of researchers, for some reason mostly Germans. Some claimed that the gold must lie in the Hindu Kush, others that it was surely to be found in Central Asia beyond the Himalayas – this because Herodotus mentioned that camels were ridden to escape from the fierce 'ants' by those who tried to steal the gold-bearing sands. Laufer claimed that the ants' gold was to be found at the headwaters of the Yellow River in China because the Mongolian word for ants, *shirgholji*, was so similar to *shiraighol* which means yellow river.

Another German scholar, C. Ritter, claimed that the ants were marmots and that the land of gold must be up the Sutledge River in the central Himalayas. These locations were thousands of miles apart, and none of the identifications was either convincing or conclusive. Entire books and countless pamphlets had been published on the subject of the gold, yet it had never been found.

All these theories were summarized in 1938 in a scholarly book written by a German, Professor A. Herrmann. Herrmann believed that the ant story was no more than the product of man's imagination; he suggested that possibly ordinary ants had dug up gold-bearing sand but that the size of the ants had grown with the stories, getting bigger the further they got from the true source of the gold. The gold, Herrmann declared, must lie south of the Indus somewhere in Ladakh where gold is still found, possibly in the Suru valley where it is panned for today.

Reading on I found one scholar who held that the gold-digging ant story did not come from Asia at all but from African folklore, and that the land of the gold should be looked for in Ethiopia. Clearly the mystery remained unsolved, so that more reasonable men believed it to be a legend or a lie. I could not accept such an easy conclusion for by now I had been bitten by gold fever and had a secret theory of my own. First and foremost I felt that I should try to identify who exactly were the Dards mentioned by the Greeks and whether any of them still survived.

In my research on the Dards I came across a book by the famous linguist G. W. Leitner called *Dardistan*. It contained a map of Dardistan, its legends, customs, songs and even photographs of Dards. It seemed that they had already been identified. I feared there was nothing more to do, that I had been beaten to it. Nevertheless I decided to look up Leitner in the *Encyclopaedia Britannica*. In it I read that Leitner 'became principal of the government college at Lahore in 1864, and there originated the term "Dardistan" for a portion of the mountains on the northwest frontier, which was subsequently recognized to be a purely artificial distinction'. It seemed that Leitner's Dardistan did not exist. How strange. Quickly I turned to the letter D . . . Dar . . . 'DARDISTAN, a purely conventional name given by scientists to a tract of country on the northwest frontier of India. There is no modern race called Dards, and no country so named by its inhabitants.' The more I read of Leitner's Dardistan the more curious, yet confused, I became. Leitner, I now found out, had never seen the strange Drok-pa of Ladakh. All things considered I found it wiser to put Leitner and his theories aside for more recent references to the Dards.

Thus I came upon a brilliant article published in 1978 by the Oxford scholar Graham E. Clark. Under the title 'Who Were the Dards?' he explained that the Dards were primarily the by-product of the mania of nineteenth-century scholars for classifications. This mania, linked to what he described as naïve evolutionism' (which wished to see the world, and in this case the Himalayas, stamped by the rise and fall of classical antiquity), resulted in numerous scholars hoping to find present-day evidence of peoples mentioned by Greek scholars twenty centuries before. Was Clark perhaps speaking of me?

It is a fact that most Himalayan scholars, like myself in this book, were only too happy to quote classical masters, many of them trying desperately to match unscientific 'classical evidence' with reality in the field. From my research it soon became evident that no one had actually ever identified the Dards mentioned by Herodotus. It could well be that none of the existing inhabitants of the western Himalayas could be traced back to ancient times. Clark summed it up thus: 'Not only is it unclear as to actually which people are to be considered Dards, but the group so named, evidently contains heterogeneous peoples, with little connection other than their contiguity. The labelling of any of these people as Dards lacks firm basis . . .'

Yet if the Dards were as yet unidentified, who were the fair people I had seen at Mulbekh? I tried next to discover a little more about the Drok-pa of that region. The only person to have written about Drok-pa customs was, I learnt, the Rev. A. K. Francke, a priest at the Moravian mission in Leh, the capital of Ladakh. This mission, one of the most remote in Central Asia, was manned by several sturdy German scholars who took particular pains to record the history of the region. Notable among them was the Rev. Karl Marx (no relation), who wrote a detailed history of medieval Ladakh. As for the Rev. Francke, his vast corpus, written at the turn of the century, included several monographs describing certain customs of the Aryan Drok-pa. In the seventy years since Francke's work no one else, it seemed, had bothered much about these strange people.

I now learnt that both Francke and Marx associated the Drok-pa with the Dards of Herodotus, although they brought no proof to this claim. A similar claim was made by such modern experts on Ladakh as Professor Giuseppe Tucci and his colleague Professor Luciano Petech, although neither had made any detailed study of these elusive people whose valleys have been forbidden to foreigners since 1947.

As to the region being the cradle of the Aryan race, this now seemed to me an unreasonable claim, although closer examination did reveal that Hitler had indeed sought to mount an expedition to the upper Indus in search of 'the cradle of Aryanism'. This mission was also supposed to record sacred rites and rituals and gather any other information about the 'Master Race', but of the actual expedition I could find no further trace.

Most anthropologists agree that there is no pure Aryan race. The term Aryan is used to describe the ancient Caucasian people who spread the Indo-European languages throughout Europe, Iran, northern India and also apparently most of Central Asia nearly four thousand years ago. In the light of this one must have serious doubts as to Ladakh, or any other land, being the cradle of Aryanism. Herodotus might have been a little imaginative and Leitner inaccurate, but Hitler was certainly no anthropologist.

To confuse matters further I now came across a book written by a certain Ghulam Mahomed who had painstakingly collected local legends and stories about the Shins of the upper Indus, a Muslim people who lived around Gilgit where the Indus, on leaving Ladakh, turns south across Pakistan towards the Persian Gulf. The Shins spoke Shina, a language said to be related to the language of the Drok-pa of Ladakh. According to Mahomed these people were not Aryan at all but claimed to be descended from Arabs. 'They are probably Jews,' he continued, 'and have come via Afghanistan from either Persia or Turkey.' So much for the cradle of Aryanism.

Ever more intrigued I scanned the most obscure pamphlets on Weidner's shelves, learning that long before Francke the Drok-pa had been briefly studied by R. B. Shaw, the British Resident in

Ladakh from 1871 to 1876. Shaw, in an article entitled 'Stray Aryans in Tibet', called the Drok-pa the Arderkaro. He had compiled a small vocabulary of the Drok-pa dialect, comparing this with the Shina languages spoken around Gilgit and in the Astor valley of Pakistan. It was clear that these languages, all Indo-European, were related, even though they were not mutually understood. But what was most interesting was that the Drok-pa dialect appeared to be the most archaic of all.

By this time I had become more than a little sceptical about anything I read. No one, I realized, had ever studied in detail the strange Drok-pa of Ladakh. My only certainty was that at last I had once more found a worthwhile subject for my personal investigation – one that, if not virgin, was still shrouded in controversy and contradictions. There was, I now knew, much to be discovered about these people variously known as the Drok-pa, or Arderkaro, or Dards, or, as they were called by the man who had studied them most extensively, Francke, the Minaro. To avoid further confusion between Shins, pseudo-Dards, Arderkaro and Drok-pa I decided to adopt the name Minaro to describe the Buddhist, Dard, Drok-pa of Ladakh.

The time had come for me to set off to the Himalayas to find out who these Minaro really were.

2

CEASE-FIRE

It was late in June 1980 when Missy and I landed in Srinagar, the capital of Kashmir. Not enough differentiated us from other tourists, I felt, as we walked over to the new concrete and glass terminal. Barbed wire fences around the air strip, soldiers carrying machine-guns, and the rotating of a khaki-coloured radar scanner reminded us that Kashmir was still overshadowed by the threat of war. This brought home to us our major concern: whether we would be allowed to enter the remote valleys of the Minaro usually forbidden to all foreigners.

As I stepped into the terminal I was greeted all too soon by a familiar face, that of a security officer. 'Welcome to Kashmir,' he said with a suspicious smile. 'Please come over here and register. Are you going back to Zanskar?' he continued, still smiling; obviously the government of India was interested in my itinerary. I smiled back uneasily and signed in.

Minutes later we were rattling in the direction of Srinagar in a black Indian 'Ambassador'. Looking out of the car's window I noticed large billboards welcoming us to 'The Happy Valley' in the name of Grindlay's Bank, Bata Shoes, and Mohi Lal's Curios, Carpets and Papier Maché, billboards all but obstructing the poplar trees rising like feathers towards a deep blue sky. Suffering as I was from jet-lag and the retarded effects of the intense heat of New Delhi I looked at Missy, so serene, her dark curly hair bobbing in the breeze, and wondered if I hadn't abused her naïve confidence with all my stories of the secret Himalayas. How secret, now that every travel agent was organizing expeditions, safaris, treks and tours to the once-secluded monasteries of nearby Ladakh? Could there be anything new left to find here?

The taxi squealed to a stop at the head of stone steps that led to the edge of the dark waters of Dal Lake. As I got out, to my pleasure I spotted Muhammed, the son of the owner of the houseboat on which I had stayed during several of my former visits. He rushed forward with a broad smile on his face. 'We prayed Allah for your safe return,' he explained, 'for when you come back we make money.' I thanked him for the consideration, feeling slightly sick. Steadying the bow of the *shirkara*, I helped Missy aboard one of these oriental gondolas that taxi back and forth between the houseboats and the landing, their calico curtains billowing in the wind.

We paddled off past rows of palatial houseboats, gaily adorned with blue and white awnings flapping in the breeze on the roof terraces. These boats were a reminder of the tortured history of Kashmir. In 1848 the British had given over Kashmir, a Muslim valley, to a Hindu maharaja. Later on, his ungrateful heirs had refused to allow land to be sold to the British who sought out the cool air of Kashmir during the unbearable summers in India. As a result, unable to build summer cottages, the British constructed houseboats, grandiose versions of the local floating homes whose quaint shingle roofs surmount cedar-panelled barges. The houseboats were moored to narrow little islands, planted with yet more poplars and willows whose silver fronds glittered in the sunlight. In the water I caught sight of the purple reflection of the surrounding mountains which enclose the Vale of Kashmir, since antiquity the doorway to that secret world of inner Asia.

From Kashmir had stretched out the caravan routes that linked India with Afghanistan, Russian and Chinese Turkestan, China and Tibet. Srinagar had long been the market place for all of Central Asia. Its historical importance had been considerable even before Alexander the Great's conquest of India. Alexander himself never saw the Vale of Kashmir, but he sent some of his generals there to verify the submission of Abisares, Kashmir's ruler at the time. Two thousand years later the British had been quick to see the strategic importance of the Vale of Kashmir, to which was annexed the entire western Himalayas up to the Karakoram range so that Kashmir State far exceeded in size the ancient boundaries of the valley of Kashmir, reaching out as it does to the borders of Afghanistan, Chinese Turkestan, Tibet and India. When the British left India in

1947 disputes soon arose over the borders of Kashmir. In that year
both India and Pakistan invaded Kashmir, which wished to remain
an independent state. Later, in 1962, Chinese troops advanced on
Kashmir and settled in the far east, taking over a part of Ladakh.

The strategic importance of Ladakh, claimed by both China
and Pakistan, spelt trouble for our plans. That night I could not
sleep and sat up poring over our maps. Again I realized that the last
surviving Minaro villages lay right along the Indus where it crossed
the 1949 Indo-Pakistani cease-fire line. While parts of Ladakh had
been open to foreigners since 1975, the immediate vicinity of the
cease-fire line remained forbidden territory. This would necessitate
a special permit that only the Indian Home Ministry could grant. I
knew it would be no easy task to obtain this, but I was optimistic.
Too optimistic, perhaps.

As a result of all the years I had spent in the Himalayas I had
acquired many friends in the government, not only in Delhi but
also in Kashmir. I knew my way blindfold, or so I thought, through
the intricate corridors of the Indian administration, the most over-
staffed civil service in the entire world – an administration not only
rife with all the ailments which riddle Western bureaucracy, but one
doubled by the plagues of a caste system which further complicates
the subtle differences between an assistant sub-secretary and a
sub-assistant secretary. It was an administration whose seedy buildings smell of mouldy straw, the hallmark of so-called Indian air-
conditioning: a fan blowing through a dampened bale of straw.
This smelly, inefficient device comes as back-up to the ceiling fans
that slowly whirl in every room.

It is these fans that cause most of the disasters and some of the
accomplishments of Indian bureaucracy. They are the only things
that constantly stir in these otherwise sleepy hideouts where civil
servants seem petrified in a lethargy that dates back to the time of
Ashoka. The fans, in the meantime, do their devilish job of shifting
papers; blowing a chit off one desk and on to the next, or lazily
turning the pages of long forgotten files before gliding a vital paper
through space from one file to the next. Documents are forever
getting lost, as the fans silently pursue their mischievous duty.

Most foreigners confronted with such an administration, being
unfamiliar with the role of the fans, go mad trying to follow their

files. One of the secret weapons I had acquired over the years was lead-weighted paperclips which, if they tend to make your documents plunge to the bottom of every pile, at least have the virtue of preventing your request being blown into the waste-paper basket (the double zero of the Indian Civil Administration's roulette).

Lost in the corridors of the Indian bureaucracy I fell asleep, wondering how I had again got involved in this wretched business.

The following morning I headed for the Government Tourist Office, fighting sacred cows, rickshaws, army trucks and over-loaded buses on my way to the centre of town while Missy went over the list of equipment and stores to make sure that we had everything we would need to stay alive in the mountains.

'I can, alas, do nothing for you. You must see the Chief Minister.' This expected phrase was uttered by my friend Mr Ashraf, a member of the less complex administration of the State of Jammu and Kashmir. For every Indian state has its own government headed by a Chief Minister (equivalent on a local level to Prime Minister), which of course only helps to complicate and enlarge the already immense Indian bureaucracy.

The Chief Minister was, I knew, none other than Sheikh Abdullah, the 'Lion of Kashmir', one of the great political figures of Asia. Seventy-six years old and well over six feet tall, Sheikh Abdullah had spent more than thirty years in and out of jail for his political activities, yet he alone could crystallize and control the contrary forces that, in Kashmir, so often clash in bloody uprisings. He was a national hero, a living legend – a lion indeed – in a land torn between allegiance to Pakistan on account of its Muslim majority and to India because of its Hindu maharaja. Kashmir made repeated bids for independence as Pakistani troops invaded from the west while Indian troops poured in from the south-east.

A cease-fire was eventually called through the intervention of the United Nations in 1949. After that the heavily guarded cease-fire line was established, with Pakistan controlling the north-western portion of Kashmir, including the Karakoram range, the towns of Gilgit and Skardo, the capital of Little Tibet along the upper Indus. Nonetheless fighting periodically broke out between Pakistan and India, making this frontier the most volatile of the Indian subcontinent.

In the course of my previous expeditions to Ladakh I had become a friend of the Sheikh, and I now trusted that he would be able to give us the necessary special permit to enter the restricted zone. Anxiously I went with Missy to the Chief Minister's residence the following day. After a short wait in the company of arrogant-looking fat politicians we were ushered into the Lion's office. Sheikh Abdullah came forward to greet us with a smile. With his long pale face he looked rather like a gentleman from Boston, dressed as he was in a surgeon-type blouse and vast white trousers. Although old in years he had that young appearance that very tall men often retain, and it was evident that he was still very much a charmer, a man confident in his ability to direct others through humour rather than mere authority.

The Sheikh welcomed us effusively, expressing his pleasure with the book I had written on Zanskar and the films I had made on the area with the BBC, which he believed had been helpful in attracting tourists to his State. I winced when he mentioned them, since I dislike tourism as much as I loathe the Indian bureaucracy.

To my immense disappointment Sheikh Abdullah went on to explain that it was not within his power to grant me the permission I requested and that he would have to refer the matter to the Central Government of India. Knowing what this would entail in terms of lead-weighted paperclips my heart sank, though it rose a little when the Sheikh showed me the strong wording of his message addressed to the Indian Home Minister, stating that it was of 'the utmost cultural importance to the State that Dr Peissel carries out research in the area'.

Our interview was concluded by Sheikh Abdullah suggesting that we proceed to Kargil, 'where you should soon receive your permits'. Kargil was a trading town half-way between Srinagar and Leh, very close to the cease-fire line.

I was upset by this initial delay, but I knew that I would be able to do a lot of research in Kargil itself and I trusted that Sheikh Abdullah would soon see us in. At least it would also allow me time to return to Zanskar, a remote, Tibetan-speaking kingdom in Ladakh where I intended to make a detailed record of the numerous, ancient sculpted stones that I had previously discovered there. I believed that these might throw new light on the identity of the early inhabitants of the Himalayas during the time of Herodotus and possibly before.

In preparation for this journey I got Mr Ashraf's office to send a radio message to the single police post in Zanskar, asking that a runner be sent out to contact my old friend and travelling companion Lama Nordrop requesting him to meet me in Kargil. I then secured letters of introduction to the District Commissioner of Kargil and their Head of Police.

This done we took a taxi back to our houseboat on Dal Lake to collect Missy's list of final purchases. Whatever the outcome of Sheikh Abdullah's petition we would have to plan on spending a minimum of four or five weeks in the wild. I knew that apart from the small bazaars of Kargil and Leh we would find no surplus food, nothing to buy in Ladakh, as the local inhabitants will not sell or exchange their limited produce.

The following day we paid a final visit to Ram Kaul's general store in the old bazaar of Srinagar where flies hold a permanent convention. One by one our wicker baskets and kit bags began to bulge, with rice, dhal, onions and a few tinned foods fighting for space amidst a small pressure-cooker, tea kettle and assorted cheap aluminium pots and pans: the essentials for survival. We were at last ready to leave the Vale of Kashmir for the mountains.

It was cold on the lake when we got up the next morning. The entire staff of the houseboat was on deck to see us off, some lamenting our decision to leave, others no doubt already praying for our safe return.

One by one our heavy kit bags and baskets were loaded on to the *shikara* which took us over to our waiting taxi at the landing-stage. We then headed for the Srinagar bus station, hardly a glamorous place from which to start an expedition. In the dim light of dawn I recognized our bus among the sleeping, rusting monsters at the depot. Its dented roof and shattered windows made it look like the carcass of some prehistoric monster. Fortunately I knew that in the matter of Indian buses appearances can be deceptive: the most battered vehicles often hide the newest engines. As I inspected the interior of the bus I saw that around the windscreen blossomed a complete shrine to Guru Nanak, founder of the religion of the turbanned Sikhs whose creed lies half-way between Islam and Hinduism and whose members are known not only for their beards and turbans but also for comprising the majority of India's bus and taxi drivers.

I hate buses as much as I hate tourism and the Indian bureaucracy; indeed in India I find that I soon become very intolerant. I often wondered why. Was it because of the heat or the slow, nonchalant attitude of Indians towards life, the exact opposite of the active way of being of most Europeans – a way of being and thinking shared by Tibetans and most Himalayans, who are also impatient with the Indians of the plains. It is strange how close we Europeans are to Tibetans and yet so different from Indians, be they Hindus or Muslims. Or was I, I wondered, just prejudiced after years spent in the mountains in the company of Tibetans whose language I spoke. The Himalayas were, in a way, my second home, and one I was impatiently looking forward to seeing again.

My heart raced as, having supervised the loading of our bags, we set off at last. Though I hate buses I do love motion, the promise of excitement. I smiled to myself as we roared out of Srinagar. Three hours later, to the creak of gears, the whining of children and the rattle of the vehicle's ancient chassis, we began to climb out of the Vale of Kashmir, heading up the 11,000 foot Zoji-la pass. As we ground slowly up I peered apprehensively out of the window down a sheer 5,000 foot drop where, the preceding summer, a truck with a load of passengers had fallen. The horrendous flight had taken several minutes yet, miraculously, one man had survived. I preferred to think of other things, and so pointed out to Missy some straggly birch trees, the last we would see as we were now entering the parched, treeless void of the great Ladakhi highlands. Once over the pass there stretched before us a mineral inferno of jagged peaks, barren gullies and canyons which seemed to have been ploughed by some mad god. We were now within the high altitude sanctuary beyond the great Himalayan range, a world far apart from the Indian plains, in a territory where only the most hardy would proceed.

Before us lay the mysterious world of the Tibetan highlands, a continent within Asia, the last stronghold to have resisted invasion and cultural conquest by the West. Here I had lived out many of my childhood dreams, walking for days behind yaks and ponies in the company of monks or traders, seeking caves or camp sites for shelter, panting up endless trails leading to passes which separated each valley from the next: small isolated planets in which few foreign faces were ever seen. It was a world which looked to Lhasa as its spiritual capital, one in which the wheel was known only as an instrument of prayer, a world in which spirits and ghosts were thought to be as real as stones. Here every man was considered a friend, for often only a smile could ward off the stark bleakness of nature. A world of harsh contrasts which, strangely, had bred one of the most open-hearted, gay people of our planet. Yet it was also, alas, a world doomed, now encroached upon by China, India and the insidious penetration of foreign ideas. It was here that over the years I had come to be a stranger to myself; here that I had acquired not only a taste for Tibetan beer but also for Tibetan humour; here that I had felt, more than ever before, the joy of being surrounded by nothing but nature's vast horizons torn by the majesty of solitary peaks.

Peering out at the desolate landscape I hoped that Missy might get to like its eerie charm which spoke to the soul rather than to the senses. Exhilarated by the altitude I leant out of the window to catch a breath of the cold breeze laden with the scent of cut grass as we passed the first villages. How I loved these instants before arrival at a destination, the moment when all illusions are possible. How would this expedition turn out, I wondered. Would Nordrop be there awaiting us?

Soon we were rattling through the village of Dras, whose few pastures supported a mixed population of Baltis, who are Tibetan-speaking Muslims, and some Shina-speaking people who had migrated here in the seventeenth century from what was now the Pakistani side of the cease-fire line. These Shins were among the presumed Dards about whom Leitner had written and were definitely related to the Buddhist Minaro we had come to study.

Rumbling along the Dras river at breakneck speed we entered a lunar gorge, driving ever deeper into the maze of barren ranges. Hours later we came upon the surprising vision of green terraced fields like oases planted with poplar and apricot trees. We had reached the outskirts of Kargil, a lonely town whose streets were lined with box-like adobe shops which reminded us that Kargil had once been famous as the principal caravan stop and trading centre in this desolate region.

When the bus came to a halt I pushed through bags and babies to supervise the unloading of our equipment. Stepping over mangy dogs, shaking off the dust from the journey, I felt weary but happy to smell once again the musty odour of Kargil's bazaar. The fragrance of spices mingled with the sickly smell of the carcasses of recently slaughtered goats, all overlaid with petrol fumes mixed with the incense-like scent of yak-dung fires.

Kargil is both a likeable and a wretched place. It seemed to have changed a good deal in the last few years. The two original little hotels with their one common room and millions of fleas were now overshadowed by newly built shacks boasting 'Integrated plumbing – fully connected' to differentiate it from ordinary Kargil plumbing which usually failed to have any water in the pipes.

Turning my back on the prospects of a bath I headed straight for the 'dak bungalow', the government guest house, to find my friend Ghulam Muhammed Kakpori. He was, as usual, sitting on the veranda in the evening sun, but ran out to greet us. Short and handsome, with a mischievous smile, Kakpori was forever joking. He spoke perfect English, the sort of English associated only with literary pundits or those foreigners who have taken the greatest pains to master the smallest details of grammar.

Kakpori had gone to secondary school and college in Srinagar, but rather than just acquiring that habitual veneer of culture usually dispensed to young hill people he had developed a genuine interest in scholarship and research. After returning to his home valley he had not sought to make money but instead had pursued his study of local history. Recently Kakpori had been appointed Tourist Officer in Kargil to help direct the increasing flow of foreigners into Ladakh.

With its magnificent monasteries peopled by Tibetan-speaking, red-robed monks, Ladakh, understandably, became a roaring tourist attraction overnight. Nearly 10,000 people visited the region in 1979. The consequences were soon felt. Monks began selling off their rosaries, silver butter-lamps, thigh-bone whistles and other objects of worship. Assailed with doubt as to the value of their traditions, they were beginning to lose their faith. Monks by the dozen were leaving their monasteries to work for foreign money, ignorant of where such a new life would lead them.

Few tourists, however, lingered in Kargil, for the broken down buses, empty petrol drums, open sewers and corrugated iron roofs of new administrative buildings destroyed any poetry that might have been spared by the Indian Army camp. High on the hill, dominating the bazaar, white stones had been arranged on brown gravel proclaiming 'SHOOT TO KILL'; while UN jeeps were a constant reminder of the proximity of the cease-fire line. It was hardly a Shangri-la. Yet the place had its magic, that of a frontier post, a reminder that what the British had called the 'Great Game' along India's north-west frontier was not yet over. The dak bungalow, with its wooden veranda overlooking the bazaar and army camp, recalled those days dear to Kipling.

The next morning, stiff from the beds that looked and felt like tables, I strolled down to the bazaar in the cold morning light. The crowd, which must have appeared dirty and quaint to most of the foreigners, reminded me of all those ancient population movements which had accompanied the tormented history not only of Central Asia but also of the whole Asiatic world: countless migrations between east and west through the Himalayas, along ancient trade routes. Would I be able, I wondered as I elbowed my way down the main street, to sort out the mysteries of these migrations over the centuries and discover who had truly been the area's earliest inhabitants.

In the crowd I noted Turkomans with oval heads and protruding ears alongside brachycephalic Mongolians with slanted eyes. Here I spotted the thin noses of dark Indo-Aryans, there the black beard of an Afghan warrior. Further down the bazaar I observed yaks tied to the willow trees beside the river where, only a few years ago, bactrian camels from Chinese Turkestan had been tethered.

Closing my eyes I had no trouble imagining what Kargil must have been like in ancient times, when to travel you needed neither a ticket nor a cumbersome vehicle. In those days the only way to pay for long journeys was to trade along the route. Marco Polo's account of his travels is but a series of tips and advice as to what to buy here and sell there. The most famous of all Asia's trade routes was undoubtedly the great Silk Route taken by Marco Polo which linked China, across the Tarim basin, to Samarkand, and from there led to the Black Sea and Europe. The fame of this route overshadows the no less important, though little known, southern route which linked east to west, the route which runs through Kargil. Starting far away in China, it crosses the high plateaux of the neolithic herders of Tibet, eventually reaching Lhasa from where it follows the Bramaputra River to its source in the grassy plains which lead down to the headwaters of the Indus. From there, following the mighty river, it crosses Leh before continuing down the Indus to the bridge at Khalatse. There the route splits in two, one branch going south-west over the mountains to Kargil and Kashmir, the other carrying on to Skardo, Gilgit and Afghanistan. Since earliest times this southern route has been an alternative to the Silk Route between east and west, and along it have travelled many of the soldiers, scholars and pilgrims who changed the religious and political face of the globe.

Excitedly I explained to Missy how in the second and third centuries AD this was the route taken by the religious emissaries of the Afghan-Kushan rulers of north-west India on their way to spread Buddhism to Central Asia and, eventually, China. Later, in the eighth century, the armies of the early Tibetan kings had swept along this route in the opposite direction, conquering the entire western Himalayas and spreading there their language, customs and religion.

Between the tenth and fifteenth centuries the Muslims took this same route, but in the opposite direction, on their religious crusades eastwards, Kargil marking the point of deepest penetration of Islam into the Himalayas.

The first European on record to have passed through Kargil and visited Ladakh by this route was a Portuguese by the name of Diego d'Almiedo, in 1600. This simple man, a cleric and trader, was persuaded that the Buddhist monasteries he saw in Ladakh were Nestorian Christian institutions. This he reported back to the very surprised Bishop of Goa. Subsequent visitors were a Capuchin missionary in 1626 and later, in 1717, the Jesuit Deseredi, who took this route on his way to Lhasa where, for a brief time, a Catholic mission had been established.

I carried, as a guide book so to speak, a copy of William Moorcroft's *Travels to Ladakh*, a collection of notes written in 1823 by the first Englishman to visit the area. Moorcroft, a veterinary surgeon who had originally been a physician, was a keen observer. He was the first to report the strange, European-looking people who lived around Kargil. Sadly, he never returned from this adventurous journey, for after exploring Ladakh he went across the Karakoram to Khotan where he died of a fever. It was his faithful servant who rescued Moorcroft's papers, which were later published.

What endeared me to Moorcroft was that like so many Victorian travellers he stood for no nonsense. His fatherly advice was sound: '. . . if a European follows in my tracks I should strongly recommend him not to bring with him any Hindustani [Indian] servants. In the winter they are benumbed by cold, and in summer they are homesick . . . the servants for a journey in Central Asia should be Persians, Tibetans or Turanis. The first are objectionable when amongst Uzbecks on account of their Shia faith, the second are apt to indulge in inebriety, the last are unquestionably the most useful.'

Alas on my first journey to Ladakh I had not been able to lay my hands on a Turani, a man from Russian Turkestan. I had not really known what to do for servants, when the owner of the Tibetan restaurant in Kargil had introduced me to a 30-year-old, red-robed monk from Zanskar, called Nordrop. This young man had seemed as if he had little propensity for getting drunk, as Moorcroft had hinted, and since I spoke no Turani or Persian, but only Tibetan, I had latched on to him to guide me through his valley. Since then I could not imagine travelling without him.

I was now waiting for Nordrop.

3

HUMAN SACRIFICE

Two days after our arrival in Kargil, Nordrop, to my great delight, turned up.

Nordrop had pronounced Mongolian features, yet his skull was long and thin, a reminder of the mixed Mongolian and Aryan blood of his ancestors, typical of most people from Ladakh. Five foot six tall, he looked at Missy, startled, and then quickly sizing her up exclaimed, *'Pé chimbu!'* (Really tall) and burst out laughing.

'Well, what else is new?' he asked, looking up at Missy with his naughty smile. Then, as if to excuse his rudeness: 'I've brought some medicine for your soul.' And he fumbled in the interior of his dust-covered, red robe that fell just above his ankles exposing the oversized walking shoes I had given him the year before. Having produced from the folds of his robe a bottle of my favourite arak, a barley whiskey brewed by his brother especially for me, Nordrop proceeded excitedly to tell me the latest news in Zanskar.

He explained how he had received my radio message purely by accident when he passed a man on the trail who knew of my arrival. All was well in Zanskar, the great news being that the Dalai Lama of Tibet was expected there, his arrival to coincide with the official opening of the first road into Zanskar. Thus, I realized sadly, the long isolation of what must have been one of the most inaccessible valleys in the world was about to come to an end. I shuddered to think of the implications of the road for the people of Zanskar and for their culture. Overnight they would have to join the consumer society and develop a monetary economy. Doubtless the young would be obliged to leave their villages to become wage earners in the cities with which the new road would now connect them.

I tried to explain these pitfalls to Nordrop, but he was too excited by the fact that not only could he now reach Kargil by truck in two days (instead of the four or five days' walking it had taken previously) but also the new road would be bringing His Holiness the Dalai Lama.

'Before he arrives I must take you to Rolagong,' continued Nordrop. 'There you can see where we gather our medicines.' He was referring to a lonely valley full of alpine flowers where, I learnt, all the local doctors and monks went to collect the medicinal herbs that made up, along with dried frogs and wolves' paws, their amazing medical kits – a valley I longed to visit.

Having received no news from Srinagar I decided we should set out for Zanskar right away and examine there the prehistoric monuments. The next day we roared out of the bazaar in a battered truck, its horn parting the crowd before us. Thus began a two-day journey spent choking in dust and being flung around in the back of the truck as it hit every pothole that workers were busy trying to fill before the arrival of His Holiness. The dust gave us infrequent opportunity to contemplate the dramatic scenery. From Kargil we rose up the broad Suru River valley, dotted with oasis-like villages, hemmed in by cliffs leading to glittering snow peaks. Here and there the silver domes of tiny one-roomed mosques gave evidence of the deepest penetration of Islam into Tibetan-speaking territory. It was, I recalled, this valley that Hermann believed to be the home of the gold of Herodotus, an assumption yet to be proven.

The last fifty miles of the Suru River valley led through a no man's land of glaciers, falling down from a double row of peaks, the tallest being the twin summits of Nun and Kun, rising to 23,400 feet. Eventually the high cold valley opened up into a small plain of gravel, hemmed in on all sides by mountains. Here, at 13,000 feet, four torrents met, producing gravel deposits and several marshy patches surrounding the massive form of the Rangdum monastery, the most westerly bastion of Lamaism. This monastery is set in one of the coldest inhabited places on our planet, for in Rangdum it freezes every night of the year. Yet what the surroundings lack in comfort they make up for in grandeur. Rangdum is a fitting gateway to the secluded, barren, arctic valley of Zanskar, which lies beyond it over the 14,500 foot Pensi-la pass.

We spent our first night in a tent at the foot of the monastery. I was delighted at last to be back in the high mountains, where I felt so well. I now considered Nordrop almost a brother, having spent so many months over the past years in his company. Along the rugged trails of these mountains we had shared many joys and fears. We had spent many nights cooped up in smoky houses talking to old men about their land and its ancient customs. Together we had frozen in rock shelters on high passes and risked our lives as, clinging to each other, we crossed freezing torrents, always on the move. Under his guidance I had tried to understand more of that strange Tibetan world that stretches out from Rangdum two thousand miles to the borders of China.

As we sat now in the cold around our little Primus stove Nordrop told me of his latest dream, the building of a house to replace the dark one-roomed cell in which he lived. He would build it himself, he explained, when the poplar trees he had planted beside his house had grown, in another four or five years. He also had plans for building a watermill for grinding barley by the stream that ran through his village – a plan that would require him to travel eight days over the Great Himalayan Range to carry back on his shoulders over the glaciers of the 17,350 foot Umasi-la pass a piece of timber big enough to serve as a water channel to direct the stream on to the blades of the mill. Such was the scarcity of wood and the hardship of life in Zanskar. Missy listened in amazement as Nordrop spoke of his plans. Although she had travelled extensively in Europe and spoke four languages, the Himalayas were new to her and she had never before encountered such simple technology.

Missy, bruised and covered in dust, confessed that she was much more enthusiastic about driving motor cycles or riding horses than travelling in the backs of trucks. She soon took to the rigours of Himalayan life, however, dissimulating well that she had never lived rough or camped out before. In no time our tent was assailed with children and their parents who asked for pills and bandages, placing before us their cuts and bruises. The children were awed by Missy's height but soon seduced by her smile as in broken Tibetan she dished out medicines and admonishments in a desperate effort, like so many before her, to get Himalayan children to wash with anything other than mud. 'Now ta-ta-pooh-pooh,' I heard her say,

'you don't get a bandage until you wash with water, all over.'
Somehow the children understood, or at least half-understood as,
drenched in freezing water from head to foot, having washed
themselves over their clothes, they lined up for the bandages and
sweets given out by 'Ani-la', as they called her. I sensed that Missy
now knew what had brought me to love the Tibetans, a people
whose joviality and openheartedness had conquered even the likes
of Leitner, Shaw and other rigid Victorians.

The next day, in the same truck, we rumbled on in our cloud of
dust, down the western valley of Zanskar until we were dropped in
the evening at Thunri, Nordrop's village. Thunri is composed of a
cluster of some thirty whitewashed houses made of adobe bricks in
the Tibetan style with small, latticed windows. Zanskar, one of the
world's highest valleys, is under snow for six or more months of
the year. To survive, its inhabitants have to retire in winter to
cave-like underground rooms with no windows, so that they can
keep themselves warm around fires of yak dung, the only fuel in
this treeless land. The few trees that do grow near the villages are
planted and irrigated with the same care that we in the West reserve
for flowers. Nordrop, in preparation for building his dream house,
had planted several poplar trees in a small rocky enclosure beside his
present house. It was in this little 'forest' that we set up our tents.

We were woken the next morning by the voices of children
leading the village sheep out to graze, their cries echoing above the
roar of the brook that ran beside our camp. Opening the flap of my
tent I could see the summits of the Great Himalayan Range rising
right up from the other side of the brook. Here at 13,000 feet the air
was crystal clear, allowing us to distinguish rocks and glaciers miles
away, outlined in jet black shadows as those cast by the sun on the
moon. The north face of the Himalayas, located in the mountains'
rain shadow, is an arctic desert with one of the most rugged
climates in the world.

I wondered what had brought man to live in such an apparently
desolate place. Had he been driven here by force (as the theory goes)
from better climes, or was he simply attracted by the austere beauty
of the place, oblivious of hardship? For to live at such an altitude
was never an easy task. It would take us lowlanders six weeks to
acclimatize fully. Great heights not only require a long period of

acclimatization but ideally call for special mutations, adaptations to the thin air such as are found among the Peruvian Indians. The Tibetans, unlike the Incas, do not have special enlarged lungs or physical attributes any different from those of other Mongolian peoples. Yet their typically Mongolian broad noses help the Tibetans heat the cold air they breathe, while their hands and cheeks, fat and well irrigated, are designed for cold climates. Was there once, here as in Peru, a true native, a Himalayan? This was one of the things we had come to find out.

As soon as we had recovered from our harrowing ride, which was twice as tiring as walking, Missy and I began looking for carved stones. We set off to the foot of a cliff just above Thunri where, previously, I had found a large boulder carved with figures of ibex. It portrayed a whole herd of ibex facing two human forms with bows in their hands; near the bowmen were several dogs, apparently barking at, or rounding up, the ibex. This naïve scene was carved into the rock by the method known to prehistorians as 'pecking': a tool, possibly another rock, was used to hit the rock, pecking out minute chips which eventually formed the design. The ibex were simplified, not to say stylized, while the men were depicted as if drawn by children. But despite their simplicity these images displayed a certain classical elegance.

Ever since the age of 12, when I had copied a picture of a bison drawn thousands of years before on the wall of a cave, I have been fascinated by the work of Stone Age artists. I am always struck by the perfect rendering of their animals which proclaims that prehistoric man had a definite sense of style and good taste. This was visible here, too, in the heart of the Himalayas.

As I re-examined the stone I could not help feeling that the images must have had some special significance. What could it have been, I wondered? Why a hunting scene, and why at this spot? And who had drawn them? My inquiries and studies had revealed that similar engravings of ibex were encountered with certain frequency in Tibet, Ladakh and northern Pakistan. Professor Tucci states that 'carvings of this type are so common in Asia, however, that we cannot draw any valid conclusions about their origins or about the interplay of influences between one area and another.' This comment I found somewhat unimaginative, for I certainly believed that these pecked stone carvings were of the greatest antiquity, and therefore must inevitably have some bearing on the early history of the Himalayas.

Tibetan prehistory must be one of the most secretive and obscure fields of scientific endeavour. The reason for this is that Tibet and the Himalayas have been closed to foreigners for so long that even the study of modern Tibet had yet to be fully undertaken. I became interested in its prehistory by accident, in the course of my first expedition to the Himalayas in 1959. Having found myself stranded at the frontier of Bhutan, Sikkim and Tibet, I was invited to visit a mission outpost in Lepcha country, and it was there that for the first time I heard of Asian 'lightning stones', prehistoric artefacts which the local people believed to have fallen from the sky. There I was shown a small collection of polished stone axes, frozen thunderbolts, believed to have come down from heaven. I was then taken to the foot of a tree which had been struck by lightning, at whose base the tools had been found. Beside it was a pit, perhaps the mouth of a cave. It was not long before I was climbing down looking for more tools.

Drawings of ibex, similar to those I now encountered, are common in European neolithic and earlier mesolithic caves; in fact 30 out of 165 caves of that time in Europe have ibex figures. From the lower paleolithic period onwards, for many thousands of years, ibex were hunted by man all over the globe as one of his favourite prey. Representations of ibex are numerous around the world, although ibex themselves are now very rare.

In Zanskar I lost no time in letting it be widely known that I was particularly interested in such carvings of *skin*, as ibex are called in Tibetan. Soon friends of Nordrop's were having me run left and right to examine various drawings of ibex, all within a hundred yards of the village. This ibex hunt led me further afield, panting up to the high pastures several hours' walk from the village where real ibex could still occasionally be seen.

I began taking photographs of the stones, hoping that maybe one day I should be able to date them. This, of course, is difficult, for although we now have a revolutionary series of new dating techniques such as oxygen isotope and calcium carbonate records, or potassium argo and uranium-disequilibrium dating methods, there is no sure system for establishing the dates at which a rock might have been pecked or carved. It is presumably possible to establish some sort of chronology for rock oxidation, although I imagine that each type of rock must have a different rate of deterioration.

It all seemed a hopeless task, and one that I was about to give up, when I noticed that many of the stones with ibex hunting scenes were drawn over with the sketchy outlines of *chortens*, the well-known domed Buddhist monuments, pecked out of the rock in the same manner as the ibex, but on top of them. These *chortens* varied in shape, some with simple circular domes set upon a platform, others more elaborate structures with staircases rising to domes, like an inverted top, crowned by a spire.

Might this not be a clue? There was no doubt that such *chortens* were of very ancient design and in some cases probably dated back to the earliest days of Buddhism, some possibly stretching back to the first century AD, to the time of King Kanishka, the Aryan ruler of north-west India. This was apparently confirmed by the local belief that King Kanishka had founded the first Buddhist institutions in Zanskar. I noted with interest that the outline of these ancient pecked *chortens* was generally of a much lighter colour than the outlines of the ibex hunting scenes they covered, which seemed to prove that some of the ibex carvings were definitely well over two thousand years old. Yet this gave little indication as to why and by whom they had been drawn.

Discussing all this with Nordrop in Tibetan around a kerosene stove in our mess tent, I tried to explain to him my interest in the Stone Age and how keen I was to find out who had lived in Zanskar many years ago. Of course Nordrop had a ready answer, for he knew well the tale of the creation of the world, common to all Tibetans. This told how in the beginning Tibet was a vast lake, which had slowly subsided. At first there were no men, only monkeys that lived in caves. One day these monkeys went to a turquoise lake where they found a goddess, with whom they had intercourse. From this union were born the first men. 'You see,' explained Nordrop with a smile, 'our ancestors came from caves, just as you were explaining to me.' I had tried to give Nordrop some idea of our own theories about neolithic man, explaining that long, long ago in Europe people had also lived in caves. Nordrop was delighted that we both agreed on this point, for he believed to the letter what his religion had taught him. A devout Buddhist, he had spent most of his life in the monastery at Karsha, as attendant to the Chief Steward. As such he had been in charge of collecting grain owed to the monastery by the various families who leased monastic lands. As a result of his collecting activities Nordrop knew every village and nearly every household in Zanskar.

'Zanskar is covered with ibex stones,' Nordrop explained to me as he prepared our evening meal. 'But why bother to look for them all?' I had trouble explaining to him. Indeed I was not certain that I fully knew myself why I was so irresistibly drawn to Stone Age artefacts. I was always surprised by how little we actually knew about our origins. I had been fascinated a few years back by the discovery in the Philippines of a new Stone Age tribe. Mesmerized by their faces, I sought in them an answer to all my questions about our own origins.

Of course I knew that there are still many Stone Age survivors on our planet – the Bushmen, the Andaman Islanders, and certain aborigines from Australia and New Guinea, to name a few. In the 1900s there were still three tribes who did not even know how to make fire: the Pygmies of the Congo, the Andaman Islanders and the Tasmanians all used fire but could not make it themselves. But however revealing the study of these peoples was, they all belonged to races and cultures quite different from those of ancient Europe and so shed little light on our own European ancestors. Who were those men who left us so many magnificent cave drawings, and the no less fascinating standing stones of Stonehenge and the stone alignments at Carnac in Brittany? Who had erected the solitary menhirs which still stand guard over the landscapes of England, Ireland, France and Spain, silent sentinels mourning a past about which we know so little? I yearned to know why these stones had been erected, and even more I wished to find out what the builders of such structures believed in. If our Stone Age heritage in Europe is rich in artefacts it is poor in traditions, although some ancient traditions do survive, as Frazer points out in *The Golden Bough*. In rural Europe certain rituals and customs are still laced with the last strands of neolithic memory, doomed no doubt to be soon stamped out by the demands and turmoil of modern life.

Yet traces do exist – tales of tree spirits, unicorns and fairies, the worship of oaks and other trees, strange taboos, and dim memories of human sacrifices – the last ghosts of a world swept away not only by barbarians but also by Christianity which, like Islam, had little tolerance for pagan beliefs. Buddhists, all told, were more tolerant than either Christians or Muslims, so that in Zanskar, as through-out Tibet, no effort had been made to suppress or destroy mement-oes of the past.

Examining the ibex carved rocks I wondered why there were so many drawings of ibex and not of other animals. Did the ibex have a special meaning, and if so what was it? Ibex, like rams' heads, are one of the oldest 'religious symbols' I realized, as I recalled their use in other cultures. Probably the goat horns first used by man with a sacred or religious connotation were those found in Russia at Teshik-Tash. There they were laid out, surrounding the body of a child buried in the foetal position. What is remarkable is that this child was believed to be Neanderthal, which makes the grave one of the earliest examples of human burial rituals in the world.

At a much later period a goat head with long horns became the dominant artistic theme of the earliest Chinese pottery and bronze ware. Stylistic in a fashion that strangely foreshadows later Mayan art, the goat head symbol, called Pao Tie, decorates many of the three thousand year old Chinese Shan bronzes.

Ancient Chinese manuscripts tell us that the earliest barbarians of Tibet, long before the establishment of the Tibetan Empire, revered the wild horned sheep, *Ovis hodgsoni*, also known in the West as *Ovis amon* – a strange coincidence since in Egypt and Greece, Ammon, the Sun God, was also symbolized by a ram. 'Son of Ammon' was one of the many titles Alexander claimed for himself. As such, he is often represented with rams' horns, the famed 'golden horns' of the Macedonian King. It seems unlikely that there is any direct link between the role of the ram's head in the cult of Ammon and the ancient Tibetan and Central Asian rever-ence for wild sheep. Or could there be?

In the course of my travels all over the Himalayas I had frequently found rams' heads nailed above the doors of houses or on the porches of chapels. They are considered protectors, 'those that stop evil', by the local inhabitants. In Mustang I had witnessed an elaborate ceremony for the chasing of evil spirits from the kingdom's walled city. Prayers and chants were offered continually for three days so as to trap the spirits in the web of complex antennae-like threaded sticks placed in offering plates. Once the evil spirits had been coerced into these traps they were taken out of the town, the traps were destroyed, and the evil spirits supposedly fled in the form of a goat. This was but one of the many forms of the ritual of goats taking away evil. In our vocabularies we all have a term for this: in English it is scapegoat, the ram that takes upon itself all evil, which finds an echo in the Lamb of Christ who takes upon himself the sins of the world. Does this image spring from some neolithic cult, I wondered.

Nordrop, Missy and I began to travel around the villages that dot the central Zanskar valley. At night, after long chats over buttered tea and meals of curried rice cooked by Missy over yak-dung fires, we slept on the floors of the houses of Nordrop's many friends.

Along with ibex drawings we found many standing stones. The most spectacular of these lie a few hundred feet west of the monastery of Sani, considered to be the oldest monastery in the land. These stones form a ring; the tallest of them is ten feet high, although it must be larger as it is partially buried in the ground. Long after they were erected, this tallest stone and some of the others had been carved with crude figures of standing Buddhas which had been somewhat deformed to fit the odd shapes of the rocks.

These standing stones in Zanskar are a hint to the ancient link that may have united the Himalayas with Europe of old. The first scholar to discover such a link was George N. Roerich. In 1925 this amazing man, scholar, mystic and painter, led a scientific expedition with his son into the wilds of Central Asia for the purpose of exploring the 'nomad graves' of Chinese Turkestan, the Altai, western Mongolia and Tibet. There he discovered that in ancient times a great part of Asia that I and most people had presumed always to have been inhabited by Mongolians and Tibetans, had actually once been inhabited by a long-headed people whose skulls he found in various tombs. These people were, it seemed, descendants or relatives of the ancient Scythians from the area around the

Black Sea whose 'animal-style' gold objects form part of the famous treasure of the Hermitage Museum in Leningrad. Roerich found that some Tibetans still had these distinctive animal-style designs on many of their possessions such as stirrups, knives and the pouches in which they kept their tinder and flints for making fire.

More surprising still was that Roerich and his son found many tall standing stones, or menhirs, similar to those found in Europe dating from neolithic times. At Do-ring near the Pang-gong salt lake they found an important alignment of eighteen parallel rows of stone slabs, menhirs, running east–west, ending in a cromlech of two concentric circles of menhirs surrounding three more standing stones and a stone altar. This huge monument in the heart of Tibet was remarkably similar to that of Carnac in France, having, to quote Roerich, 'precisely the same arrangement'. He also found several other large alignments and standing stones scattered all over Tibet.

Who had built these monuments is a mystery yet to be solved.

It was Roerich's research that had led me to think that Tibet might hold many more clues to the nature of our ancestors, because if elsewhere ancient traditions had long disappeared, here and in the Himalayas they had been protected by the tolerance of Buddhism for archaic beliefs. Moreover, in the course of my expeditions to Mustang and Bhutan, while absorbed in other studies, I had frequently found traces of the ancient past: standing stones, cliff dwellings and rituals of a strange pre-Buddhist religion still practised over much of the Himalayan world. Then there were all those standing stones and carved boulders which we had now come to study. In Zanskar we found over thirty standing stones, some alone, others in sets of three – monuments similar to those found in Europe and those discovered by Roerich in Tibet, testimonials to a long forgotten civilization and religion whose mysteries we now wished to elucidate.

In Zanskar I discovered that ibex were drawn on the kitchen walls in every house at the New Year. The drawings were made with white barley flour, dabbed on to the smoke-blackened walls in the same style as on the ancient rocks. They were thought to bring good luck. I found out too that in funeral rites in Zanskar little images of ibex were buried along the route by which the corpse was carried out of the village to be burned – 'so as to assure that the spirit of the dead does not return and haunt the village'. All this was very interesting but it hardly explained the great number of ibex drawings I encountered. Professor Petech suggested that the ibex might once have been an object of worship, but the drawings we found had little in common with figures of worship. The ibex were never depicted oversize or set upon pedestals or surrounded by an aura or halo, but were generally pictured in groups or small herds, frequently being hunted with dogs and bows and arrows. Missy actually found a representation of men hunting them with slings; as she remarked, this is hardly the way to treat a divinity.

We were still at a loss as to what to make of these carved stones when we reached the fortress-like village of Konchet overlooking the central plain of Zanskar in which lies Padum, the home of one of the two kings who have long ruled this remote region. At Konchet we came across a remarkable shrine. It was a 'cleft rock', a large pointed boulder which was split vertically in two. This I found particularly interesting since I knew that in ancient times split rocks had been held in awe throughout Europe where they have given their names to localities. There are accounts which claim that such rocks were split not by frost but by lightning, and this would link them to the stone axes and arrowheads which in Europe, as in Lepcha country and Tibet, are often believed to have issued from lightning. The cleft rock at Konchet was covered with ibex hunting scenes, which seemed proof that such drawings must have had at least some religious significance.

Even more interesting was that the cleft rock of Konchet was topped by a *latho*, an altar to the local mountain god. All over Tibet and the Himalayas, in every village, one finds traces of a mysterious, ill-known, very ancient, pre-Buddhist religion. It is often referred to as the 'religion of men' in contrast to the Buddhist 'religion of gods'. In all appearances it seems to date back to neolithic times. It is characterized by local gods who inhabit the mountain tops and are considered to be the owners of the soil. Cairns and standing stones were set up in their honour, often topped with goat or ibex horns, sometimes those of yaks and also with juniper branches. Little more is known of this ancient religion, other than that these gods of the soil were held to be able to bring about rain, to protect the crops, and to be generally concerned with man in his relation to the land. They were placated with juniper smoke, or the sacrifice of sheep and rams, and, until recently in eastern Tibet and other areas, young children. Boys of 8 or 9 years old, it had been explained to me, were once sacrificed to these gods in Zanskar. The strange 'religion of men', whose origins remain very much a mystery, is nevertheless adhered to by thousands of farmers and herders who still render homage to the local land-owning gods at their numerous shrines.

The local mountain god worshipped at the cleft rock of Konchet resided, we were told, on a lofty peak on the other side of the central Zanskar valley from Konchet. Could there be a link between the carved ibex on the cleft rock and the ibex horns which adorned the shrine to the god of the soil? I began to fear that maybe I would never find an answer to these mysteries. I might have to conclude, like Professor Tucci, that 'we cannot draw any valid conclusions about their [the ibexes'] origins'. As we made our way back to Thunri I felt depressed by our lack of progress.

Such was my state of mind when that evening the burly, one-eyed village headman came and sat by our fire. We were talking about ibex as usual when he said, point-blank, 'If you are interested in ibex and the Drok-pa why don't you go to Hameling?'

Hameling, I knew, was a small village set high in the western extremity of Zanskar, on the road to the Pensi-la pass; a village which we had passed on our way in from Kargil. I had now travelled into Zanskar four times over that route and remembered Hameling well, having sampled some excellent barley beer there. The village struck me as unremarkable, nothing but an ordinary Zanskari village with a door *chorten* in the midst of a cluster of a dozen or so houses set among barley fields at 13,000 feet.

'Yes,' continued the headman, 'they say that the name Hameling comes from Hanu-ling.' Hanu was, I knew, one of the three main Minaro villages on the Indus. I had the man repeat himself twice.

'Everyone knows they are Drok-pa, although some of them are ashamed to say so.'

To my amazement, Nordrop confirmed this.

'But why have you not told me this before?' I asked him. He had not remembered, he claimed, explaining that there was not just one Drok-pa village in Zanskar, but three. The largest, he said, was Gyagam, while the third was called Remala.

'Let's go there immediately,' I exclaimed, for I had received in Thunri notice from the District Commissioner of Kargil that so far there was no news of my permit to go to the other Minaro villages near the cease-fire line.

Thus it was that at dawn the next morning we prepared to set out for Gyagam. I hired a pack pony to carry our equipment, arranging that Missy should ride Nordrop's grey mare. We then folded up our large blue mess tent and smaller tents before sorting our provisions, for we wanted to leave some behind in Thunri. To help in camp and to guard our things we decided to take along a young boy called Che-wang, whose smile all but split his broad face. For him this journey was a true adventure, since he was as keen to live close to foreigners as we were to discover more about local customs.

As we plodded on up the western branch of the Zanskar River, dwarfed by a hedgerow of glaciers, I kept saying to myself over and over again, 'It must be a mistake.' There could not be any Minaro in Zanskar. Were we not a hundred miles away from any of the 'known' Minaro communities which lay on the far side of the great Zanskar range, a range whose lowest pass was over 16,000 feet high? Furthermore Zanskar was an old, well established, Tibetan-speaking principality populated by Mongolian-featured descendants of the great Tibetan invasions. Indeed the Zanskari dialect of Tibetan was much closer to the language of central Tibet than the dialects of the rest of Ladakh. Surely the Drok-pa referred to by the headman in Thunri and by Nordrop were not Minaro but plain Tibetan nomads, maybe from nearby Rupchu, the high plateau east of Zanskar, or from the northern plains of Ladakh where rough nomads similar to the American Indian, Mongolian-type nomads of the central plains of Tibet still lived – people who were certainly 'very primitive' but unmistakably of Mongolian stock. I was all the more sceptical because the Rev. Francke, who in his enthusiasm for the Minaro seemed to find traces of their culture everywhere, stated in his *History of Ladakh* that 'Zanskar has apparently never been colonized by Dards [Minaro].'

As we walked slowly between the snow peaks, Nordrop and I plodding on to the tinkle of the bell of Missy's pony, I realized how long marches are most conducive to thought. My mind raced over all my memories, trying to imagine the world as it must have been thousands of years before. Little would have been different in Zanskar: the mountains, the climate, the flora and fauna would have been the same. But what about men? Had they lived in caves or stone shelters, or even in houses? There is little reason to believe that earliest man could not have put wood and mud together to make shelters. I reflected that we often give too little credit to our forefathers, forgetting that a skilled artist who can draw animals can certainly use his hands and brain for less delicate tasks. There is no scientific reason to believe that neolithic man was any bit less intelligent than us, and it is a modern conceit to regard artists as less able than mechanics. How strange too that we rarely seem to consider the soul of Stone Age man, depicting him instead as a sort of glorified ape. Surely this was a mistake, a Western snobbery, the same that led the Victorians to consider the wearing of shoes as a sign of civilization.

It was four o'clock when, having passed the village of Remala, we reached Gyagam. Missy was exhausted, afflicted as she was by a serious problem with her knees which made climbing painful. I only discovered this when I observed that once she got on a horse she never got off. This had surprised me, for if there is one thing really uncomfortable to sit on it is a Tibetan saddle, a rough wooden frame whose protruding angles are barely smoothed over by piles of old carpets and blankets. I who had spent so much of my life in the saddle could hardly endure more than a couple of hours before having to get down for a very necessary walk. The Tibetans have a proverb that a horse which cannot carry its rider up a hill is not a horse, while a man who rides down a hill is not a man. I could not blame Missy for not being a man, but I did find it strange that she clung willy-nilly to her saddle, uphill and downhill, all day long. Such was her pride in hiding her problem that she only once complained, and that was not about her knees but of 'fanny fatigue'.

We had decided to set up camp in Gyagam, as this was the largest of the three so-called Drok-pa villages. But when we reached it we found that most of the houses looked rather run down and the people, at first sight, none too friendly. Seeing this I decided to pitch camp above the village behind a little chapel, backed against a clump of straggly willow trees. This Nordrop called a forest, and indeed the trees were a pleasure to behold in the otherwise treeless landscape of parched scree slopes rising up to rock cliffs which merged into the tall mountains whose glittering peaks towered over us.

Our camp was well above the river, at 13,300 feet. Looking down the valley from our tents we could see below in the distance the outlines of the whitewashed houses, like sugar cubes, set in the sharp green of their oval barley fields. Zanskar, I thought again, must be one of the highest agricultural communities in the world. In many villages the crops did not even have time to ripen before the onset of winter; where that happened, the barley would be harvested when it was still green.

I was too busy putting up our tents, and later too tired to strike down to the village again that night, so I sat on the wall that enclosed the 'magic wood' of Gyagam and peacefully watched the sun set on the far peaks. I had previously encountered 'magic woods' only in Bhutan. There they were considered to be the residence of the gods of the soil. I wondered whether there was some relation between the two, the ancient beliefs of Tibet and those of the Minaro.

That night I could hardly sleep for excitement. If it were really true that the people here were related to the Minaro it would mean so much to my quest. To begin with, it would matter less whether or not I received permission to go to the other villages. It would also confirm that the Minaro had once lived over a much vaster area than was previously believed. Such a discovery would change the entire picture as to the origins of these people.

4

A STONE AGE ARTIST

The following morning I was awakened at dawn by Nordrop's droning voice as he recited prayers from the worn little book he always carried wrapped in a silk handkerchief tucked into the folds of his robe. Nordrop's piety always came as a surprise to me. There was nothing sad or sombre about his approach to religion, no contradiction in his mind between his outgoing mischievous character and the tenets of his faith. The witty, critical comments which accompanied his sharp eye for human weakness were matched not by pity but by warmth and understanding.

I was pleased to note how well he and Missy got along, his openness and good humour matching hers as he teased her about her pronunciation of Tibetan words. Nordrop had come from a poor family and had had to struggle to survive after his father's premature death, working for richer monks by carrying loads and doing their errands, and at the same time studying to master the intricate Lamaist doctrine. He brought this same enthusiasm to our quest, finding it more amusing than serious, thinking no doubt that we were mildly mad while himself becoming slowly infected by our madness. Hitching up his robe he would run around inspecting boulders for ibex, when not busy chatting up and cross-questioning old people and learned monks in the hope that they might reveal a little of the store of their amazing collective memory which bridged a thousand years or more. In a medieval land such as Zanskar I came to appreciate that the Stone Age was just around the corner. No economic or social revolution had come to interrupt the long chain which linked them to the past. But was Nordrop's past linked to Tibet or to the West, I wondered as I heard him shout '*Julay*' (Good morning) and add with a laugh

'Come come, *mémé!*' – *mémé* meaning grandfather, the term that I used to tease him.

Thinking of breakfast I remembered that for all his virtues Nordrop was a lousy cook. The night before, when Missy had been too exhausted to supervise our dinner, he had served up a glutinous rice afire with chillies. Food was the last of Nordrop's concerns, for he himself was content with huge servings of dry, parched barley flour wetted with a little buttered tea. Butter, for Nordrop, was like caviar; his eyes would light up every time he opened, with great care, the bladder skin in which he kept huge chunks of the precious rancid stuff. I was forever holding him back from dropping some into our tea or chocolate. He would shake his head in despair, smiling as he drank his greasy broth alone. I ran over quickly to stop him from throwing anything into our breakfast that morning.

Huddled over the Primus stove I sharpened my pencil for a day of inquiry. I did not have to wait long, for all too soon five little children were pushing and shoving in front of the door of our mess tent trying to catch a peek at the strangers who had camped in their village. Immediately, and with great delight, I noted that none of them had Mongolian features, although they all had dark eyes.

My wildest expectations were soon confirmed when two men from the village walked up to our tents. I bade them sit down and began questioning them in Tibetan, with Nordrop translating when necessary into their Zanskari dialect.

While they talked I examined their appearance. The men had long faces with thin, straight noses and eyes which were almond shaped with not a trace of the epicanthian fold which is characteristic of most Mongolians. They wore rough, homespun *chubas*, vast robes like dressing-gowns with sleeves so long they have to be rolled over to reveal the hands. These *chubas* hung nearly to the ground and were a burgundy red colour, wrapped at the waist with a somewhat brighter red cloth.

These men confirmed that there were three Drok-pa villages on this side of the river, adding that there were two new small settlements on the opposite side populated by an overflow of people from the right bank. They claimed that they originally came to Zanskar from the Minaro settlements on the Indus, although they said this happened 'hundreds of years ago'.

Pointing above the village of Gyagam to a vast ruin, they explained that this had been their fortress. Yet they could not recall any of the names of their rulers or leaders, declaring that they now had no king. They told us how there once had been a very cruel chief of the Drok-pa, 'Gyalpo Pong Kham', which literally translated means King Donkey Foot. The story went that King Pong Kham was very ill-tempered and would beat everyone until the villagers became desperate, and were at a loss as to what to do. In the end they made a huge fire and then all sat around it, inviting the king to join them. When they were all sitting there quietly someone shouted, 'Look, look, there comes a man!' The king turned to see, upon which the villagers immediately grabbed him and threw him into the fire. The next morning, in the ashes, they found what seemed to be the footprints of a donkey and so deduced that their cruel king had indeed been an animal. This story was said to be a legend, but as a case of regicide it was unusual although quite characteristic, I soon discovered, of the Minaro's love of independence.

To commemorate this event annually the villagers of Gyagam, on the 21st day of the eleventh month, at the time of the great 'New Year's celebration', make huge fires in front of their houses. Then men and women congregate around these, speaking only in the Minaro tongue.

One of the men went on to confirm that the villagers of Gyagam were truly blood-brothers with the people of Hanu, having come here fifteen generations ago to hunt ibex. They had eventually built three villages, first that of Hameling, then Gyagam where we were and last of all Remala, the next village down the valley.

At first few of the people I questioned admitted to speaking Minaro (an archaic form of Shina), but slowly, as I loosened their tongues, I learnt that all the adults could speak relatively good Minaro.

While I was conducting my interviews Missy went off. She returned a few hours later, greatly excited. 'The place is just littered with carvings of ibex,' she exclaimed. 'I photographed dozens and there are many, many more. Come and see.'

That afternoon we spent climbing behind the sacred wood to the top of a gigantic fan of rocks and boulders which poured down into the Zanskar River below. It is on the lower half of such spills of scree that most of the villages of Zanskar are built. Following the cliffs which bordered the far side of the spill, Missy led me to dozens of large rocks with carvings pecked out on their smooth rust-brown surfaces. Ibex were the most common representations, but here and there we noted not only hunting scenes but also what seemed like battles, men with bows and other unidentifiable weapons. Certain stones were covered with as many as fifty images of ibex with great sweeping horns. Here and there very primitive *chortens* had been carved in the rocks over the ibex, as if to proclaim the hold of Buddhism over whatever ancient cult these ibex scenes might have represented. Similarly, in Europe, one often finds crosses carved upon ancient standing stones as one belief superseded another.

I was most excited by this massive find, but also puzzled – not only by the quantity of stones but also by the fact that some of them appeared to have been carved only recently. As we returned to our tent I was pleased to discover several more carved stones around our sacred wood, while just behind the wood stood two *lathos*, rectangular piles of stone forming altars to what I then believed to be the gods of the soil of the 'religion of men'. Not far from these, to my surprise, there stood, as in Konchet, a large cleft rock embedded in the wall which surrounded the sacred wood.

That evening I continued my interviews by candlelight in the frail shelter of our mess tent. There was now no doubt that we were in a very old Minaro settlement with a people quite distinct from the other inhabitants of Zanskar – people who spoke a dialect of Shina and practised, as I was about to see, many of the rituals and shared most of the taboos of the Minaro of the Indus valley. In fact the only marked difference was in their dress. Here the Minaro men all wore the long traditional Zanskari homespun robes, while the women wore the spectacular but strange local *perak*, a head-dress with two protruding 'ears' of curly black sheepskin separated by a broad leather band on which are sewn dozens of turquoise stones and coral beads. These head-dresses constitute the entire dowry of the women. I knew that the women of Dah, Hanu and Garkund, villages of the upper Indus, favoured instead an equally strange,

Phrygian type of bonnet, worn not over the head but folded flat and placed on top of the head. This bonnet they ornamented with needles, coins, ribbons and dried flowers. On the other hand the Zanskari headdress, like the Ladakhi, is very similar to that of the Kailash of far away Kafiristan, the only tribe of Pakistan to have escaped conversion to Islam.

I now asked my new Minaro friends about the carved ibex stones; did they know what they represented, who had made them, and why they had been made? At first, I received evasive answers such as 'Who knows?' and 'They are very old and that was long ago.' By now I was fairly experienced in prying information out of country people in the Himalayas; I knew one should never take no for an answer and that patience was usually the best solution. It was evident that the inhabitants of Gyagam felt somewhat ashamed of talking about their pagan traditions before Nordrop, a monk of the Buddhist faith. Although the Minaro of Zanskar all claim to be Buddhist Lamaists they are not very ardent disciples of the Lord Buddha. Whereas in the rest of Zanskar there was at least one, if not two monks to every household, there were but two monks in all of Hameling, one in Gyagam and two in Remala. In all only five monks for over forty households, a very small proportion indeed for a land with so many monks and monasteries.

Slowly, as I gained the confidence of the more enlightened men of the village, I started to collect more information about the settlement. They explained to me that originally the Minaro settlements had been camps for ibex hunting. The three villages of Hameling, Gyagam and Remala had as their divinity a certain Babalachen (literally translated from the Tibetan as 'Father Tall Mountain'). Babalachen was believed to live up on the highest snow-covered peak on the other side of the valley. The main *latho* which I had seen above the village was dedicated to him. All this sounded, at first, to be in the true ancient 'religion of men' tradition, not very different from the old beliefs encountered all over the Tibetan Himalayas. But then they told me that they had a second shrine to a divinity called Abi-lamo, 'Grandmother Goddess', also known as Mu-shiring-men, *mu* or *mun* in Minaro meaning 'fairy'.

The villagers explained that the real vocation of the Drok-pa people had always been to hunt ibex. At Hameling, the first settlement in this valley, they had originally lived in caves. This made me sit up. In the same casual voice my informers then explained that before they had bows and arrows their ancestors used to chase the ibex over cliffs. This difficult task they achieved by making traps. I had the man repeat himself. 'Yes, *before* the bow.'

He elaborated. 'We had to chase the ibex over the cliffs. To do this our ancestors would build wooden contraptions, somewhat like waterwheels, and set them on the edge of the cliffs. When driven by the hunters to the cliff's edge the ibex would jump out on to the wooden spokes of the trap which would turn over under their weight, throwing them down the precipice, Of course this was very long ago,' concluded the man.

My heart nearly jumped out of my chest. Very long ago . . . if this was not the understatement of all times! Surely I had misunderstood. I knew full well that bows and arrows were known to the Scythians at least three thousand years ago. I thought there must be a mistake. No one could remember that far back; collective memory surely could not recall in detail techniques so old. In the West we have speculated that before man invented the bow he had hunted with axes, skull-crashers and spears but that traps were generally limited to later civilizations. Certainly some people had driven bears and other animals off cliffs, but to drive the ibex, one of the most agile of all goats, to its death would indeed be impossible without the aid of some ingenious device such as a large spinning trap. My first reaction was one of disbelief. How could they have built such a wooden trap in a land without trees? Could it be that in those days there were lots of trees in this region, where today there are none?

Thinking all this over I felt that I must have misunderstood, that it was all a fanciful invention. But the same story was repeated again and again to me and substantiated later by Minaro in Kargil. The only variation was that some said the traps were made by placing a flat stone over the cliff's edge, balanced on two other stones. When the ibex jumped on the slab it would tilt the animal over the cliff to its death, after which the stone would automatically swing back into its original position. Such details I found too precise not to believe, nor could I imagine how or why several quite different people would invent such similar stories.

But my surprise had only just begun, for now I not only established beyond doubt that the three villages of Gyagam, Remala and Hameling were Minaro settlements along with two other villages on the other side of the valley, Bacartse and Marutse, but I also began slowly to ascertain the true origin of these Minaro whose traditions seemed to extend beyond the frontiers of history.

First I learnt that except for the villages on the other side of the valley which paid ten rupees a year to the monastery of Rangdum, the Minaro villages, unlike all other villages in Zanskar, did not work monastic lands or pay taxes to the Lamaist monasteries, being treated as 'independent' with regard to local religious institutions. Was this an inherited privilege or an acquired one? The answer to this question was crucial in order to determine whether these sites were settled before or after the Tibetan settlements in Zanskar. Local beliefs confirmed the former hypothesis; an old monk told me that tradition had it that Hameling was the oldest settlement in the area.

Questioning the men further about ibex I learned that they were all believed to be under the dominion of a unicorn ibex but belonged to the Queen of the Fairies, Mu-shiring-men, who owned the wild flocks with Babalachen. I also came to learn how the Fairy Queen, as owner of the ibex, must be placated by hunters. Before men set out to hunt they had to purify themselves by passing their bodies over the smoke of burning juniper branches. This smoke is considered both a spiritual and a physical cleansing agent by the Minaro. (Legend has it that once most of the high Tibetan plateau was sprinkled with juniper trees. This is probably a fact, for still today one may encounter here and there in certain remote parched regions between Zanskar and Ladakh stands of juniper trees and some solitary trees struggling to survive.) Having cleansed themselves with juniper smoke the hunters, to please the Fairy Queen, had to abstain from having intercourse with their wives the night before the hunt. The men, who hunted in groups, would spend the night together after having offered little ibex figurines, made of butter mixed with barley flour, to the altar of Babalachen, the god of their sacred mountain.

'Goats' milk butter, of course,' explained one of the men. I now heard of the Minaro's startling taboo. The Minaro, both in Zanskar and on the Indus, consider cows to be impure. They never drink cows' milk or eat their flesh; they even have to purify themselves if they accidentally touch a cow when ploughing their fields, usually with 'borrowed yaks from [non-Minaro] neighbours'. In fact the Minaro consider cows to be the most impure of all creatures, never raising or breeding them. This taboo extends to not using yak wool or any sort of cowhide, so that even the soles of their shoes are made from goats' hide. The Minaro also abstain from burning cow dung, a real hardship in Zanskar where it is the main source of fuel.

What a strange taboo for a people technically residing in India, a land where all cows are held sacred. The Minaro's hatred of the cow I found both fascinating and disturbing, the latter because the Minaro were said to be Drok-pa, herding nomads. Today all Central Asian nomads, from Tibet to China, prize their cattle highly, especially the yak and yak-cow crossbreed called *Dzos*. The yak is the camel of the Tibetan and Central Asian highlands, the most useful of all local animals. It is hard to imagine the herders living without them. From the yak they derive not only their wool for making blankets, bags, tents, ropes and harnesses but also milk from the *dri*, as the female yak is called. (Yaks' milk and cheese is as impossible as cocks' eggs.) They also eat yak meat, as well as using yaks as pack and riding animals. One could almost describe the nomad culture of Tibet as a yak culture. Local legends are full of stories about monstrous wild yaks, considered as noble if somewhat dangerous beasts.

As I continued to question my informers I discovered that most of the men of Gyagam, Hameling and Remala did not strictly observe the taboo regarding cows' flesh or drinking their milk. As a result these men were considered impure by their own womenfolk. The women actually used separate hearths, or a separate hole in the hearth to cook their food, which was always cooked and served in different utensils from those used by the men. This meant that some women had to cook two meals, one pure and the other impure! The women, however, avoided touching the men's cooking pots which the men had to wash themselves.

Of course what interested me most was what the local people had to say about hunting ibex. The mountain god, owner of the ibex in Gyagam, had to be placated by purification before a hunt took place. In most Minaro villages, I later discovered, he was replaced by a feminine divinity, Queen of all the Fairies. The hunters had to be ritually cleansed so that the Fairy Queen should not get angry when they shot her ibex. The fairies, everyone knew, used the ibex to carry their provisions. This was confirmed when the villagers would find a grain of barley in the wool coat of the ibex or discover saddle sores on their backs, proof that at night the ibex worked for the fairies.

'How do you hunt ibex?' I asked one of my new friends.

'Oh, we mostly use guns but some still use bows and arrows, some have crossbows. Most families still have at least one traditional bow although some modern bows are made of wood; but the really good bows are made from ibex horn.'

When my friends had left I retired to think over all that I had just been told. I did not yet know exactly what to make of the information I had gathered. What excited me was that it seemed certain that these Minaro must be the descendants of the aboriginal population of this region because ibex, of whom they made such a case, are native to the area and not found in great numbers elsewhere. Indeed today they are found only in the Himalayas of Kashmir and to the east, over the northern part of Tibet.

I wondered what to make of their so-called 'memory' of how their forefathers had hunted ibex in the days *before* bows and arrows. Maybe the account of their traps was just a legend, for other Minaro had explained to me how, at the beginning of time, men had the feet of goats and could run so fast that they could catch the ibex with their bare hands. Seeing this the Fairy Queen made humans grow big and clumsy feet so that they were obliged to invent other ways of catching the ibex. Yet even such a story only confirmed the ancient ibex-hunting vocation of these people, a vocation that seemed confirmed by my further investigation as to the dominant role of the ibex in all their traditions and rituals.

I discussed all this excitedly with Missy. She, like myself, felt that maybe we were really at last getting closer to discovering who the Minaro were.

'What about the stones carved with ibex?' she asked. 'Did you ask who made them?'

'No,' I confessed, 'I completely forgot.'

The next day I got up early and wandered about the sacred wood examining the two shrines and the nearby drawings of ibex. It was a fine day and I could see miles down the valley and out over to the peaks which lined the high summer pastures along the snow line, just below the glaciers. It was easy to imagine how once the entire valley had been one vast pasture with few or no fields. Here, beyond doubt, had grazed huge flocks of the same ibex which, in lesser numbers, can still be found today high up in the mountains.

Ibex, I had been told, can become quite tame, and occasionally in the highlands they have been known to graze alongside domestic sheep. What had been the relationship between the ancient hunters that had carved some of these ibex stones and their quarry, I wondered. Recent ethnological speculation has suggested that primitive man as a hunter may have lived in harmony with the herds of game he stalked. It could have been that the ibex hunters of old followed a specific flock of wild goats somewhat as the Lapps still follow reindeer herds, or Eskimos the caribou. Maybe neolithic man had spent his days watching the ibex graze, only going out to hunt one when hunger warranted it. Maybe he had been very relaxed about the whole matter, quite unlike our traditional image of primitive man racked by hunger and fear. After all, the hunters had taken time off to peck the rocks with the elegant drawings of their prey. Archaeological remains in Europe had shown that camp sites in hunting days were visited every season in a regular fashion that seemed to be not a panicky search for game, but part of a well organized routine.

Towards ten in the morning Tsewan Rindzing, whom I discovered to be the most erudite of the inhabitants of the village, came up to our camp. Tsewan was a short man with a pointed face and weather-beaten skin; later I learnt that he was the local Labdrak, or servant of the local god and goddess, a priest of the strange ancient Minaro religion about which I had yet much to learn.

I lost no time in asking him about the ibex carvings.

'Oh,' he said casually, 'those are done after we go hunting. They are done in thanks; they are given to Babalachen, the mountain god.'

'But surely you don't still make such carvings?' I asked in disbelief.

'Yes, certainly, although we now very rarely hunt ibex.'

'But,' I protested, 'some of these carvings are very old, very very old.'

'Yes, very very old,' was Tsewan's only comment.

I could not completely believe what he had told me and so had him repeat it again and again. 'After going hunting,' he explained patiently, 'one makes a picture of the chase, in thanks for good luck. This we give up to Babalachen, the god of good luck, owner of the flocks and ruler of nature. When we have good luck and catch an ibex we also place the horns on the altar of Babalachen or on the one of the goddess of fertility, Abilhamo, whose shrine is next to Babalachen's.'

A short while later Tsewan showed me how to carve the rocks. In one hand he picked up a stone and with precise accurate knocks etched out an ibex. 'It's simple,' he declared. 'First you hack out a flat X, then two legs by joining the tops of the X passing down through the bottom; you then add the other two legs after which you do the head, tail and two horns. Always in that order.' Surely, I felt, I must have been the first person to receive such a lesson in

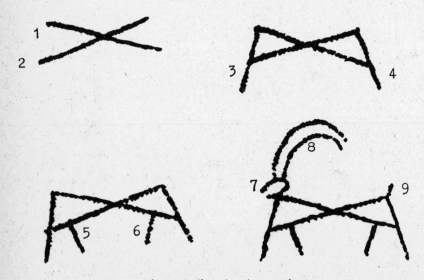

How to draw an ibex in nine strokes.

48

ancient rock carving – a lesson all the more fascinating because the ibex that Tsewan had drawn was in exactly what is known to prehistorians as the 'bi-triangular style' observed in neolithic and Bronze Age pottery and rock carvings. I was having a stroke by stroke lesson in the most ancient art form of all times. By some uncanny trick the ibex drawn in this manner are all very vividly lifelike and elegant, regardless of how one draws the initial X.

It was still too early to fathom the full implications of this discovery. Here were a people who still carved ibex on rocks; and now I knew the reason for these carvings. I had, as it were, a key to understanding not only local ibex drawings but maybe also the most ancient carvings which go back to prehistoric times. Excitedly I continued to question Tsewan in detail about how his people hunted. Did they once have stone arrowheads, I asked rather naïvely. 'Oh yes, long ago. We often still find them in the mountains along with old metal arrowheads lost years ago.' This statement, which sounded reasonable, nevertheless surprised me for it differed from the belief held in all other Himalayan areas and much of Europe, that ancient arrowheads made of stone, steel or copper are magical lightning stones which fell from heaven. According to Tibetan and Mongolian folklore lightning stones are held to be the arrows (thunderbolts) thrust by the Dragon of Thunder who romps around the heavens. But to the Minaro of Zanskar there was nothing magical about these arrowheads, they were simply old artifacts lost by their ancestors. The most ancient past and the present formed here one and the same world!

Quite unexpectedly we had now found not only a large Minaro settlement in Zanskar which had survived through the centuries but we had also been able to link their traditions with the most popular prehistoric art form of the entire Himalayas, the carving of ibex. This meant that we had discovered a white Himalayan people with neolithic traditions, possibly linked to our own European neolithic past. The implications of our find were staggering. This was, of course, far too important a discovery to be accepted without further proof and investigation. So much had already been written on the local people which was false or incomplete that we could not hastily conclude that we had found the last neolithic Aryans in Asia. The Minaro might well prove to be a foreign people who had adopted the neolithic customs of some older population. Yet somehow I felt I had found my first serious lead to identifying for certain the Dards of Herodotus.

The following morning I set out above the village to examine the fortress of Gyagam. It was partially in ruins. In vain I combed the rubble looking for carved ibex or other designs or inscriptions. I could make out the massive walls of five chambers which seemed to have few openings. One side of the building had fallen down to the valley floor over the vertical cliff on which the fortress stood. The nature of the building confirmed its original purpose, one of defence.

As was explained to me later when I returned to Gyagam, 'When armies or bandits were sighted, a fire was lit and everyone around rushed to the fort for protection.' The valley was constantly being sacked and overrun by its quarrelsome neighbours. In the nineteenth century alone, Zanskar was invaded over a dozen times, to say nothing of the incursions of small-time bandits. This seems to explain why, to this very day, in Zanskar all the women carry their dowries on their heads, sewn on to their *peraks*, which they wear even when working in the fields. I was always amazed to see them toiling away bearing their heavy turquoise and coral orna-ments, overdressed for many less-than-fancy chores. The reason I now saw was that in the case of attack they could at all times run to the fortress directly, as their savings were secured fast to their heads. The only drawback to this security system was written on the brows of many women: through the years their heavy head-dresses had rubbed a bald patch on their scalps.

The following day I visited the ruins of another fortress, at Hameling, which held a commanding position on a steep hillock dominating the upper Zanskar valley. Once the entire village had been built upon this hill, in whose caves, I was told, the early inhabitants had lived. The fortress had been destroyed by an invad-ing army from Mandi, a region on the southern flanks of the Himalayas, probably at the beginning of the last century. An old man, Tashi Norbu, swore that one could still see in Mandi the treasure of Hameling, stolen from the fort's chapel. The fortress had not been rebuilt because from 1846 the British had extended their 'protection' as far as Zanskar, although no British envoys or representatives ever lived in the valley.

Now, with the greatest regret, we had to leave these Minaro settlements. The impending arrival of the Dalai Lama would, we knew, put a complete end to the availability of both ponies and camp-helpers. Even Nordrop made it quite clear that he for one would not miss, be it for a minute, the Dalai Lama's visit. But first, on the way back, Nordrop wanted to go to the remote Rolagong valley, the vale of flowers, to collect medicinal plants. We bade goodbye to our new friends, promising to return.

5

THE KINGDOM OF
WOMEN

Leaving Gyagam we climbed for two days up the sheer, seemingly endless slope which led to the snowbound 18,120 foot Rolagong pass. No foreigners, we were told, had ever before tried to enter this valley. As we slowly gained height a parched treeless landscape opened around us, with bare vistas stretching to the horizon. Why was it, I pondered, that I so loved this barren landscape. Could it have been that such mountainous country was my natural habitat? Could it be that somehow, over many thousands of years, I had become programmed to a certain type of landscape? I remembered Tashi, my Tibetan companion on my journey to Mustang, saying to me over fifteen years previously, 'Grass and water; that is happiness.' I did not agree. I do not have the heart of a plainsman. I hate green. I suffocate upon rich prairies. I loathe cows. My body and soul, I felt, was conditioned to sweeping, arid vistas, preferring the rugged mountainscapes where ibex live.

At last we made it over the great pass, Missy, at times in much pain, being helped by Nordrop when she could not ride. We then descended into a panorama of eroded cliffs and endless bone-dry ranges with jagged teeth biting the horizon.

Rolagong was land's end, the limit at which the mountain goats had grazed. Yet here, even at 20,000 feet, the snow melted in summer to water pastures which held over 300 different alpine flowers, every one known for its medicinal properties. Knowledge of these is derived from countless years of observation, handed down by every successive generation of mankind. Thus many of the facts we know today about plants may have been passed on from earliest man in a chain stretching perhaps over 30,000 years, or 900 generations, time enough to experiment fully with each plant.

Missy Allen at the camp above the
village of Gyagam, overlooking
the barren landscape of Zanskar.

Lama Nordrop, our companion,
guide and friend.

Top: Buddhist *chortens* carved over an ibex-hunting scene at least 2,000 years old. *Centre:* Hunting with a crossbow, drawn by a Minaro within the last 100 years. *Bottom:* The author studies a carved boulder.

Donjé Nacugya *(right)*, a Minaro from Garkund, next to the village chief of Thunri. The contrast between Mongol and Caucasian features can be seen clearly. *(Photo: M. L. Allen)*

A Minaro girl and an old man. Both look strikingly European. *(Photos: H. Singh; M. L. Allen)*

Missy, riding her yak, on the summit of Rusi-la with
Sonam and Tashi.

Herodotus' 'gold-digging ants': marmots on the
plain of Dansar. *(Photos: M. L. Allen)*

Having bought medicinal plants from an old man, the lone inhabitant with his wife of this wild valley who made his living by collecting the various herbs, we climbed back out of the vale of flowers in the midst of a snowstorm. Both Missy and I were pleased to have experienced that rare privilege in our time, that of having trodden new territory. But I was troubled by a nagging anxiety about when the chain of memory, linking Rolagong's solitary resident with the past, might be broken.

Once back in Zanskar we were caught up in the preparation for the Dalai Lama's visit. Although I rejoiced with Nordrop in this great honour, since over the last four years I had come to think of myself as a Zanskari, my enthusiasm for Zanskar and its people had now been superseded by my fascination for the Minaro. It was strange to see that over the years Zanskar, like much of Ladakh, had become 'Tibetanized', so that today it was a Tibetan of Mongolian blood who preached the faith in a valley where, nearly two thousand years ago, Buddhism was first advocated by the Aryan King Kanishka to, no doubt, an audience of white-bearded Minaro.

The modern government of Kashmir, naturally sensitive to matters of religion, had gone to great pains to prepare for the arrival of the Dalai Lama to a region only just emerging into the modern world. Electric generators were being carried in for the first time along the new road. Water pipes, a novelty, were laid down to reach the Dalai Lama's camp, erected around a newly built chapel from which His Holiness was to preach. This camp was set up on the open plain in the centre of Zanskar, an arid flat land with but little grass. In no time trucks had ripped up the grass and churned up dust. Every day the howling winds sweeping down this 13,000 foot high valley blew up massive sandstorms that soon blinded the faithful pilgrims and made life miserable for everyone.

Immediately it was declared that the land gods of the 'religion of men' had been offended by such preparations for the Dalai Lama, in which they had been forgotten. All the monks present were asked, with the Dalai Lama's approval, to make offerings to these divinities, 'owners' of the soil, at shrines in villages all over Zanskar. The gods being placated, it was hoped that the sandstorms would soon abate. They did not. Yet the incident illustrated well both how tolerant is Buddhism, and Lamaism in particular, towards ancient pagan rituals and how still very much alive is this ancient cult.

In spite of the dust, the meeting was a great spectacle to behold. On foot, mule, donkey, pony or yak, from every hamlet of Zanskar, the entire population, old and young, had come down to attend the ceremonies – more than 5,000 people dressed in long maroon homespun gowns, their finest, the women stooping beneath their heavy, flamboyant head-dresses. All sat before the tented platform upon which, draped in saffron robes, rested the Dalai Lama, surrounded as if by a sea of turquoise scales which glittered in the sun as the women bowed their heads. Overcome with joy, old women grabbed my arm to explain how they were ready and happy to die having seen with their own eyes His Holiness. For five days on end the Dalai Lama explained the finer points of the doctrine of tolerance and wisdom. The front rows at his feet were occupied by over 1,500 monks from the surrounding monasteries, close-shaven, red-robed, statue-like figures chanting in a pious drone their verses, seeing their lifelong devotions crowned in one week.

As a reincarnation of the great compassionate Avalokitsevara, the Dalai Lama is more than the spiritual leader of the Lamaist Gelupa order and political head of Tibet, he is also the god of pity and mercy, he to whom those in need cry out. No words could record the intense love, hope and piety of the crowd, one the likes of which it would be difficult ever to assemble again. This was the ultimate tribute of a feudal land to its traditional values. Nothing in the crowd betrayed the existence elsewhere of a modern world, at this the final homage of a forgotten people to their living god, on the eve of their entering the twentieth century. As I watched the trucks rumble in a cloud of dust across a landscape which until then had known nothing but the roar of streams and the dust of hooves I wondered whether their creed would survive. Sadly enough, in the wake of His Holiness the Dalai Lama merchants with goods from India had come to Zanskar and were soon doing a brisk business selling the Zanskaris their first Western clothes.

Looking at the crowd I once again marvelled at the manner in which Tibetan Lamaism, in spite of its complex, demon-ridden rituals which seem to obscure the purer tenets of Buddhism, has in fact achieved in its followers a degree of piety unequalled in any other faith. Here the people, be they monks or peasants, truly practise what is preached to them, avoiding the pitfalls of 'too much or too little', respecting the old and the learned, having patience and kindness for all, men or beasts. Few modern nations have achieved such a degree of civilization in its true sense. Alas, kindness and virtue are weak weapons with which to oppose the encroaching aggression of Chinese Communism or that more insidious influence of modern ethics, disguised here not in a sheepskin but as a Dacron sweater sold by hawkers.

When the Dalai Lama had left Zanskar and the dust had settled once more I proceeded back to Kargil with Nordrop and immediately informed my friend Kakpori that we had found a Minaro community in Zanskar. Kakpori now told me that he had only recently recorded an old tale from the Suru valley which mentioned that three so-called Drok-pa 'nobles or kings' had set out from Rongdu, a region on the Indus, west of Skardo, still partly inhabited by Shina-speaking people, presumably similar to the Minaro. The tale went that in the ninth century a certain Khiva-Khilde went to Zanskar via Lamayuru (a monastery not far from Khalatse on the Indus), then into Zanskar where he built forts at Hameling and later at Gyagam and Remala, as well as one down the Suru River at Kartsé. This same tale told that the entire area was then already peopled by Minaro.

When several visits to the local police station and the District Commissioner's office had produced no news of our long-awaited permits, I decided to stay on in Kargil and collect information about the Minaro of the Indus valley from any of those Minaro who might come to trade in Kargil.

I soon found myself pacing the bazaar in search not of kerosene or supplies but of Minaro – Minaro from Dartzig, Garkund, Hanu or Dah, villages set in three small valleys which opened into the upper Indus near where it entered Pakistan. Distinguishing a Minaro from a Mongolian-looking Ladakhi was not very difficult; what proved much harder was to single out a Minaro from the many Western tourists who, for various reasons, preferred to wear the local costume. This 'going native' shocked some of the die-hard colonial types, of whom many are still found in India today. (Personally I never had any desire to go native, perhaps because I never did like Japanese in top-hats and saw no reason why they should find me attractive in a kimono.) Yet however well disguised these young Europeans might be, however well they may have wrapped their turbans, or *dhotis*, or *chubas*, one could always pick them out from Asians a mile away. Europeans have a particular way of walking, of holding their heads, and a special way of letting their arms dangle or flap around which gives them away even to the most untrained eye. A second look into their faces and one can immediately spot that greyish white mobile skin which, however suntanned, hangs on their faces (mine as well) in such a way that is never encountered in the East.

If the Minaro of Zanskar had seemed European in features, while not in dress, the Minaro of the Indus looked exactly like Western hippies. With their second-hand clothes and great bunches of flowers on their heads they looked really wild, and to be truthful at times embarrassingly ridiculous – embarrassing because they actually resemble some of one's own relatives, the sort of cousins or uncles one might be ashamed of. There is, beyond any doubt, an *air de famille* which singles them out in any crowd as alien to the modern Himalayan and Asian world.

I now found myself pursuing every scruffy, European-looking person I spotted in the bazaar. I have never been good at talking to complete strangers and am much less expert at picking up men. But now I began to prowl the bazaar, ready to pounce on any Minaro I might encounter. Somehow sensing this, perhaps thinking my intentions were dishonourable, my potential victims all managed to bolt away as I closed in on them, disappearing before I could make contact. Having repeated this manoeuvre several times, I was beginning to feel that I risked being picked up by the police as some sort of satyr. Suddenly I spotted a Minaro with his child, a small dirty brat with a fresh flower in his cap. Reviving my predatory tactics I approached him and his young with slow sideway steps until I had them cornered. Recalling the proverbial gambit of less honest prowlers I thrust a sweet into the brat's hand, thus making my first 'accidental encounter'.

'Are you a Minaro?' I asked his father rather stupidly in Tibetan, while his eyes shifted as if he expected me to have been followed by the police.

'Yes,' he replied.

'Very good,' I answered, while searching my pocket for another sweet which I again thrust on the child. 'How very nice. I'm a friend of the Minaro,' I continued, trying to look sincere.

Little did I know that the Minaro, like most Europeans, are a suspicious lot, devoid of that naïve confidence typical of most Tibetans. Saying *'Julay'* with a broad smile my Minaro, with his son still sucking the sweet, turned and walked away.

I had to do better next time, I thought. However hard I looked that morning I could not find any more Minaro, the bazaar being full of useless strangers, including a horde of French girls clad in shorts who spoke in that noisy jargon tourists always feel compelled to use abroad. I continued past sombre-looking German tourists who intermingled with Zanskaris, Purig-pas, Baltis and people from Dras. I saw a few Tibetan refugees, a Sikh bus driver, two gymnosophists in loincloths, a Bengali baboo, two Hindu army officers, a Gugarati *harijan* and several Kashmiri merchants, but no more Minaro.

In the end, as it was getting late, I gave up the chase and went over to inspect some grapes which were being sold at one end of the bazaar. Kargil is in the very heart of the highest land mass of our planet so I was truly surprised to see grapes here. For a moment I hesitated. Should I buy some and risk the agonies of tummy trouble? Weeks in Zanskar had given me a sweet tooth. The last fruit I had seen were some dry Kargil apricots I had purchased a month earlier. Fresh grapes proved irresistible. I bought some – minute, green, baby grapes the size of blueberries. The dilemma was now whether or not I should wash them, local water probably containing more bacteria than bazaar dirt. I decided to wipe the grapes clean on the lapel of my shirt, and I was busy performing this operation when along came my Minaro, eyes shifting, his child in tow playing with the wrappers of the sweets I had given him.

Moving towards me with a suspicious smile, the Minaro said *'Rash.'* With my mouth full of grapes I just stared, looking stupid.

'*Rash, rash,*' he repeated.

Quickly my mind raced through my Tibetan vocabulary. '*Rash, karé ré?*' I said, spitting out the pips.

'*Di ré*' he replied, pointing to my bunch of grapes.

I had made contact and learnt a Minaro word; *rash* meant grapes. I had also met, by the same token, Dorje Namgyal and his son, both from the village of Garkund.

Dorje Namgyal, 'Thunderbolt King of the Sky', was a Tibetan name, which was hardly surprising for the member of a race which, in the eighth century, had lost the war against the Tibetan invaders and subsequently partially succumbed to Lamaism. It was a good typical Tibetan name, but there ended Dorje's link with the Tibetan world. For him, as for me, Tibetan was an alien tongue, one which he had mastered better than I though he still considered it a foreign language. His long nose, shifty smile and pale eyes acknowledged our kinship, My heart warmed to him. For twenty years in the Himalayas I had been the victim of countless jokes aimed at my long nose and had been nicknamed 'yellow eyes', as the Tibetans call Europeans. I had full sympathy for Dorje Namgyal with his really long nose and pale eyes.

Before I could open my mouth Dorje put me in my place. 'I know we look alike,' he said, in a slow deadpan voice. I nearly choked on my grapes. I later appreciated that every Tibetan, Ladakhi or Indian they came across must have lost no time in telling the Minaro how strange they looked. You cannot, I suppose, be mocked for your looks without looking back to your relatives with amused connivance. In fact Dorje Namgyal was fed up with people – Indians, Ladakhis, Kashmiris, Sikhs, Bengalis, Zanskaris and even tourists – all telling him that he looked funny, that he looked English, or worse, like a tourist. And now I had been chasing him, in truth, because we both had long noses.

'Have a cup of tea and I will explain,' I said, leading him to the wretched hotel room in which I was camped because the government guest house, ruled over by my friend Kakpori, was full.

Having captured a Minaro I was determined not to let him go. The tea I gave him was filthy, brewed in the mica-laden grey water of the Suru River which rushed by beyond the wall of the mud hut that was my abode. I had been on the road six weeks and both Missy and I were looking a little run down, maybe a little like the Minaro.

I was feeling really embarrassed when Nordrop saved the day by coming in with cakes and a big bag of fresh apricots which the little 'Thunderbolt' gobbled up with great glee.

Once I had given my victim more tea with goats' milk, and had sent Nordrop out to get yet more apricots, I felt ready to begin.

'Well,' I asked, 'have you heard of the Drok-pa villages in Zanskar?'

'Oh yes,' replied Dorje. 'You know once all of Ladakh and Zanskar were Minaro.'

'Perhaps,' I said, recalling the severe attacks which had been levelled at the Rev. Francke for claiming, a little too hastily, to have identified Dard colonies all over Ladakh. Dorje muttered something but I was too fascinated by his ears to listen. One of his ears had three button-like discs sewn through it, while on the other hung a pendant representing the sun and the moon. I did not want to embarrass my friend by asking why he wore those strange earrings, any more than I would have dared ask him why he had a bouquet of faded flowers strapped to the top of his cake-tin-like cap. Instead I began asking questions about his village.

'How many families,' I asked, 'are there in Garkund?'

'Forty households,' he replied.

'When was it founded?'

I now heard from Dorje a tale about the earliest Minaro similar to the one I had been told in Zanskar – how they had first lived in caves and hunted ibex which, before having bows, they drove over cliffs. I managed to get more details about their cliff-edge traps which, this time, were said to be made of stone. I was then given an account of how the Minaro had first reached the district in which they now lived. The story went that seven men, coming from Gilgit, reached the upper Indus while hunting ibex. An arrow shot had led them to the lower valley of Dah, and on arriving there one of the hunting party found a grain of barley in his shoe and suggested they plant it and return later. This they did, and having found that the barley had grown well, they decided to settle in a cave. Later they built the village of Dah, which – maybe not incidentally – means arrow in Tibetan. When this first village became over-populated they founded Garkund, and later Dartzig.

Thus began the first of many sessions with Dorje Namgyal, who was soon joined by several of his friends. Every day I gathered as much information as I could about the Minaro of the valleys of Garkund, Dartzig and Dah. All these Minaro, like those in Zanskar, understood my Tibetan. Nordrop, now well trained over the course of four years to cross-check my finds and examine my informers, helped me enlarge our sparse knowledge about these remarkable people.

One of the first tasks I had undertaken was to write down a large vocabulary of Minaro words. To my knowledge the only available record of their unusual language was that compiled by Shaw, the British agent who had lived in Leh. Shaw's vocabulary contained a mere 180 words and was first published in 1887. I now tabulated 500 new words, recording their exact pronunciations on tape. This I hoped might help linguists to establish more clearly the difference between Minaro and other forms of Shina spoken in Chitral, Astor and Gilgit, and to determine for certain which was the oldest language.

I always marvel at the persistence of languages which seem to outlive variations in religion, racial type and, most of all, politics; especially our Indo-European languages which have spread over such a vast area of the globe. Certainly there are infinite variations and many different dialects, but the roots remain unchanged. Today Sanskrit and Latvian are in many ways practically identical. Some of the Minaro words I wrote down made me jump with surprise. *Shaitan* – devil; *mi* or *miou* – my; *darr* – door; *hath* – hand. 'How do you say knife?' I asked Dorje. '*Cutter*,' came his reply. *Strap* means reins, *tem* means time, and so on.

Other words were similar to French – *tu* for you, *baston* for stick – while many words had Greek-sounding endings. On the other hand some Minaro words were borrowed directly from Ladakhi-Tibetan, just as many words had been borrowed from the Minaro. This is of course one of the reasons for believing that the Minaro had once spread far afield eastwards, right up to western Tibet and possibly further.

'What is the word for ant?' I asked Dorje casually.

'*Rui*,' he answered.

'And gold?'

'*Ser*,' he replied, *ser* also meaning gold in Tibetan.

Then point-blank I asked, 'Do ants collect gold?'

'What?' he asked, surprised.

I then tried to explain the story of Herodotus but received only a blank stare. No, neither he nor any of his friends had heard of such a wild tale as that of the gold-digging ants. There was gold, he explained, as everyone knew, along the Indus but there was no story about ants digging it up. I comforted myself that maybe Dorje and his friends in Kargil were too young or uneducated to know of such a tale. When we had our permits I could ask others, much older, about this story.

As the days went by I continued to offer Dorje and his friends tea, which became rather boring. Commenting on this, I learnt that the Minaro of the Indus make wine. Beer from *rash*, explained Dorje with a twinkle in his eye.

'*Rash chang*,' grape beer, I echoed, my mouth watering. Dorje my brother! I wanted to hug the man as I told him how my country was the true land of *rash chang*. I explained that we had hundreds of varieties in France and that we drank almost nothing else. I told him how I yearned for *rash chang* and that in spite of my twenty years' affection for the Tibetan-speaking peoples and their *chang* I would, any day, exchange *ne change*, Tibetan barley beer, for even the smallest bottle of *rash chang*.

By this time I had come really to like the Minaro, whether they were the rough, primitive Zanskari Minaro we had discovered, or the more smiling wine drinkers from the Indus. A marvellous people, I thought, as one day I ran into crowds of them in the bazaar. They were in their best attire on their way to greet His Holiness the Dalai Lama on his return from Zanskar – an Aryan tribute to the Tibetan Buddhist faith. Among the crowds were groups of beautiful, fair-skinned girls with grey eyes, long hair and dreamy looks. On their heads rose delicate arrangements of fresh flowers mingled with silver and coral brooches and beads. The women wore short embroidered tunics over long, surprisingly modern, narrow woollen trousers decorated with geometric designs. Their trousers contrasted with the long gowns of the Balti and Ladakhi women, recalling that like the ancient Scythians, these women were excellent riders.

Only too soon I found out that the dreamy looks of these frail girls were quite misleading. Minaro women, I discovered, are ferocious – true witches, in fact. Just as Dorje and his friends had been soft-spoken and helpful, their women were loud-mouthed and aggressive, some women actually giving their men a whopping slap on the face in public. It is therefore not surprising perhaps that the Minaro inhabit an area the ancient Indians called Stirajya, the Kingdom of Women, also known as Suvarnagotra, the Race of Gold.

Could this have been the same place as the mysterious land of 'the women-ruled Samartans', the eastern Amazons mentioned by Herodotus? And was it just a coincidence that the Chinese also mentioned a Kingdom of Women, two in fact, one in eastern Tibet, the other in the western Himalayas? Could they all have been speaking of the Minaro? And what if despite Dorje Namgyal's statements the 'Race of Gold' was, as I believed, the same as the land of the gold-digging ants?

I was discussing all these questions excitedly with Missy, at the same time leafing through the long Minaro vocabulary we had collected, when a cable arrived, written in very plain English. It read: *Doctor Peissel is not to proceed, repeat, not to proceed to the Dah, Hanu, Garkund area.*

Thus ended our first expedition in quest of the identity of the Minaro and the gold of the ants. Bitterly disappointed, we bid goodbye to our friends and reluctantly made our way back to Europe and America.

6

THE GOLD
OF THE INDUS

Back in Boston, as I examined our notes at leisure, I could not help but feel both excited and disappointed. The excitement was that of having linked the Minaro with the ibex stone carvings. There could be little doubt that their traditions were of the greatest antiquity, that we were confronted by a people with neolithic customs, and an Aryan people at that. Here were survivors from the Stone Age, and our cousins. This was an amazing discovery in itself, but it only stressed all the other yet unanswered questions. The disappointment was that we had not yet been able with any certainty to identify the Minaro with the Dards of Herodotus, and that our permits to visit their villages had been refused. At all costs I felt I must get permission to visit at least one or two of the Minaro villages of the Indus. But how?

The opportunity arose sooner than I could have imagined, as one month after our return I received an invitation from the Indian government to travel up the sacred Ganges with a model of my latest hovercraft. These machines, remote as they were from the Stone Age, were in fact the by-product of my passion for the Himalayas. My interest in them was, in a way, my contribution to twentieth-century technology, my small contribution to the modern world which enabled me the better to indulge my passion for the past.

It had long been my dream to open up to navigation, with special hovercrafts, the rapid and hitherto unnavigable rivers of the world, an entire, natural network of communication still unused. The Ganges, issuing from the Garwhal Himalayas, was as interesting as any river for the demonstration of the capabilities of my strange craft. Two months after leaving Kargil Missy and I were back in India, this time on the banks of the Ganges.

As their inventor I loved my complex noisy machines. After all, I had been spoilt to the point of surfeit with calm, star-clad nights spent sitting around the dim light of camp fires listening to fanciful tales of demons and fairies. It was a delightful change to fight for a while the problems of cranky camshafts, flaccid skirts, lift, thrust and 'going over hump', to mention only a few of the problems involved in a new technology in which I battled valiantly with a spanner instead of a horse whip, a BMW manual instead of Bell's Tibetan grammar, and spark plugs and oil instead of my notebook and pencil.

The journey, in many respects, was a disaster. As a result of low octane petrol the hovercraft constantly overheated. We spent more time on the sweltering banks of the Ganges looking into oil filters and building cooling ducts than wallowing in the mythical splendour of the world's holiest river. In the end, when my craft broke down 120 miles from the source of the Ganges, we made it into the mountains on foot to Golmukh, the source of this most sacred river.

I had expected the source to be cluttered with shrines, ex-votos, stalls, relics and souvenirs. I thought I would find fluorescent posters of Shiva, piles of crutches, perhaps even the walking stick of Alexander. What I found was a great surprise. At the head of the world's most celebrated river there was nothing, absolutely nothing but an icy cave glistening in the sun, humming to the sound of rushing limpid water. The source of the Ganges, even approached by hovercraft, was a lesson in both humility and grandeur.

Back in New Delhi I decided that my best, and last, chance of obtaining permission to visit the Minaro villages was to go and see the Prime Minister, Mrs Gandhi, in person. For I now knew it would be useless to wander yet again through the halls of the Indian administration. Where the Lion of Kashmir had failed only Mrs Gandhi would be able to prevail over the infernal fans blowing against me.

I managed to obtain an interview for 20 November 1980. I prepared for the encounter with great excitement, for on Mrs Gandhi rested all our hopes of ever entering the Minaro villages. Dressed in my best business suit, a leftover from Harvard, I made my way with Missy through the hectic morning traffic to Mrs

Gandhi's residence. At the gate we were inspected for arms, the police taking away Missy's little Swiss army knife under the suspicious gaze of petitioners, ministers and other dignitaries. None of the onlookers could have guessed the nature of our mission, so far removed from modern affairs. Yet somehow our search for our Stone Age ancestors, a simple quest for our origins, had now got us involved with politics.

It was an unusually cool day, reminding me, as we walked across the manicured lawn to a large oval waiting-room, that the Zoji-la pass would now be closed and Zanskar, no doubt, under several feet of snow. As we waited I thought about my first meeting with Mrs Gandhi thirteen years before. I had then presented the Prime Minister with a copy of my book on Mustang and had discussed, at length, the delicate Tibetan issue. Surely Mrs Gandhi would remember our encounter. From behind a drawn curtain the Prime Minister herself now appeared, and after calling our name ushered us into a small office. Slim and erect, looking pale and austere in a black-bordered grey sari that recalled the recent tragic death of her son, Mrs Gandhi bade us sit down.

After exchanging a few words about our recent hovercraft expedition I presented her with a copy of my book on Zanskar and then referred to our previous meeting.

'Do you remember?' I asked naïvely.

'No,' she replied, point-blank.

A little shaken I then went on to tell her about our research on the Minaro, how we had recorded their languages and customs and how it was of the utmost urgency that we study the last thousand survivors of this ancient people. Would she, I asked, grant us access to their villages?

'I'll inquire into the matter,' she said, getting up rather abruptly to show us out.

It was hardly encouraging but we felt there was some hope as we headed back to the guardhouse to reclaim Missy's pocket-knife. Back at the hotel we waited to hear about our request to the Prime Minister. We waited, and waited, and waited. Every morning, our tongues yellow from an overdose of curry from the Ashoka Hotel's infamous kitchen, we called about our permits. In the end I began to wonder if Mrs Gandhi could use some of my lead paperclips. No doubt she believed that the Stone Age could wait for ever. Forty-six days after our interview we learnt that a decision had finally been reached. Permission was refused. We were terribly upset, in fact furious, not least at the expense and waste of time.

A month later we were back at Harvard, once again reduced to exploring library shelves. The books I now brought up from the bowels of the libraries seemed loaded with friendly connivance. They were all conspiring with us to rewrite the early pages of 'our' history in the East. The titles we unearthed were indicative that we were not the first to seek our ancestors east of Athens: *Surviving Scythians, the Ossetes of Russia; The Mountainous Neolithic Cultures of Central Asia and Northern India; The Neolithic Farmers of Central Asia; Racial Types in Central Asia during the Neolithic; The Central Asian Genesis of the Animal Style; Hunting and Domestication of Animals in Petroglyphs in Uzbekistan*; and so on.

What had seemed to be an obscure subject now appeared to have fascinated many scholars: Russians, Germans, Indians and Americans. Yet if we were not the first to search for the identity of the ancient inhabitants of Central Asia we knew we were on the right track. In spite of Mrs Gandhi's indifference we would go back. We would explore now the ancient gold fields of Ladakh, searching for clues to the mysterious ants. And then too we had an appointment with our ancestors in Zanskar at Gyagam, from where we would strike out into the highest Himalayas to the land of those other strange Stone Age men, the nomads of Tibet.

Regarding the Minaro of the Indus I had one last hope of entering their domain. I would appeal, I decided, to Zail Singh, the Home Minister who would soon, it was rumoured, be named President of India. Once again I solicited the necessary permit to enter the Indus gorge, determined to raise such a fuss and use so many paperclips that it could not be refused. Sheikh Abdullah would yet again, I was sure, place all his weight behind our request. 'Take Mrs Gandhi with you,' the Sheikh had said with a wry smile on our last meeting in New Delhi, when I had told him of our appointment with the Prime Minister. For years his relationship with Nehru's daughter had been strained, so it revived our hopes to read in the Boston newspapers that since our long wait in New Delhi there had been a grand reconciliation between the Sheikh and Mrs Gandhi. Maybe our chance had come.

Several months later the summer of 1981 was about to begin and we were still in Boston waiting to hear about our request to Zail Singh. I had written to all the influential people I could think of to back our request: ambassadors, ministers, even the Commander-in-Chief of the Army; but still there was no reply. The only communication we received was a letter stating that the Commander-in-Chief had retired and that a successor had yet to be named. We had no other option, I felt, but to return to India without the permit and push our request in person yet again.

So we packed our bags and the now voluminous notes we had collected on the Minaro. We were all ready to leave when Missy came back from her doctor with bad news. For years she had had serious trouble with her knees as a result of an accident, a fact which she had concealed from me on our previous expedition, clinging as she had to the saddle of ponies rather than confess her problem. Now her doctor declared that she was not to walk up even a single flight of stairs. 'Take the elevator,' her specialist had recommended, 'and in other displacements, take your car' – advice hardly compatible with Himalayan exploration. Brushing away caution, against doctor's orders, Missy insisted on accompanying me. With the help of a cane and cumbersome metal knee braces she declared herself ready for anything.

Back in Srinagar we found ourselves once again in the office of Sheikh Abdullah. The aged and then ailing Lion of Kashmir readily agreed to support our as yet unanswered request to Zail Singh, asking his representative in New Delhi to negotiate directly with the central authorities. On learning of our intention to search for carved ibex and examine the gold fields in Ladakh, Sheikh Abdullah kindly put at our disposal a government jeep.

With happy hearts, in the company of Nordrop, who had joined us in Srinagar, we sped out of the Vale of Kashmir to continue our quest for the identity of the Minaro and the location of the ants' gold. In Boston we had carefully listed all the questions yet to be answered. Were there any rituals attendant to the carving of the ibex? If so, could these in any way be linked to the monuments discovered by Roerich? Were there any other links between Central Asia and Europe? Were the builders of Stonehenge and Carnac in any way related to Central Asia's past? Though all this seemed like wild speculation I recalled that, after all, the Minaro spoke an Indo-European language akin to our own.

The wind roared in our ears as we sped in our jeep out of the Kashmir valley up the now familiar hairpin bends of the Zoji-la on to the Central Asian highlands. I immediately felt better on reaching 10,000 feet. Was it, I wondered again, that my body had been designed for this altitude, this climate and sunlight? Was this truly the land of my ancestors?

What I now had to find out was whether the Minaro were Aryans who had fled from Central Asia, or whether they were the last survivors of an earlier, white, Himalayan people whose original language had been superseded by an Indo-European one. I was thinking about the implications of this when our driver, a small seedy man with a worn jacket, slammed on the brakes of our little jeep. We came to a halt beside four standing stones set by the roadside near the village of Dras, some 40 miles short of Kargil. The stones were carved with Buddhist figures, one of which was a *chorten* which was so narrow and had been so elongated to fit the stone that it looked rather ridiculous. Here, once again, was proof that in this area Buddhism had smothered an earlier megalithic culture, possibly that of the first Minaro.

It was late afternoon when we rounded the last curve and drove into Kargil. As soon as we arrived Mr Kakpori began regaling us with an account of his visit to Garkund, one of the Minaro villages along the Indus, the previous winter. Kakpori had gone there on my suggestion to attend the Bonono festival, a celebration of thanksgiving held every three years by the Minaro. He showed us photographs of Druid-like, white-bearded men who had participated in the ceremonies, which also included a child-medium who was meant to have entered into a trance, but failed to do so. 'You had better go to those villages quickly,' Kakpori had remarked, not without irony, 'because they are rapidly losing their customs and faith. Very few still wear their traditional homespun gowns.' This I could tell from the photographs of men in large, baggy Balti trousers and oversized Western shirts. Some men were even sporting modern jackets, probably a result of contact with the Indian soldiers who garrisoned their villages.

During the festival, Kakpori explained, many songs were sung, some of which had been translated by Francke. One song recounted the nomadic migration of a group of Minaro up the Indus: how they settled in most of the villages and valleys between Garkund and far away Gilgit (in Pakistan), from where they claim originally to have come. This tale of migration had bothered me for some time, offering as it did a contradiction between the fact that the Minaro's customs linked them to the ancient neolithic carvings of Ladakh while this song claimed that they had migrated to the area from Gilgit in relatively recent times. When exactly had they come? Or could there have been, I wondered, other people similar to the Minaro in the area before their arrival? To me the simple answer was that the modern Minaro had come to resettle the area after its momentary occupation by a people locally referred to as the Monpa, 'Mon' being the term used all over the Himalayas and Tibet to describe foreigners from the south. These Mon, to me, seemed to have been Indians from Kashmir or elsewhere who had brought Buddhism to the area between the second and ninth centuries AD. Yet this recent migration was disturbing, for in order to find the ants' gold I would have to know for certain if it was indeed the Minaro who had lived in Ladakh in the fifth century BC.

All we so far knew for certain was that the life of the present-day Minaro revolved around the ibex as had the lives of the land's most ancient inhabitants who quite naturally would have left marks of their passage all over their original territory. Thus it was to search for the extent of the distribution of carved ibex stones that we left Kargil, heading for Leh and central Ladakh, following the winding military road along the Indus which ultimately would lead us close to the frontier of Chinese-occupied Tibet.

In every village and hamlet on our way Nordrop would latch on to local farmers and ask if they had seen or knew of any carved ibex. The answer was nearly always yes, although the locations of the stones varied greatly. Some were set high up on distant mountain slopes, others were right down in the villages.

Racing around in our government jeep we found an abundance of carved stones. It quickly became apparent that these carvings were of two sorts; some large boulders were literally crammed with ibex, while other, smaller stones often had but one or two animals. Here they were set in clusters, there isolated and alone. We could find no explanation for their being placed where we found them, no specific pattern or particular geographical feature which we could understand.

After two days on the road we finally climbed out of the eroded canyons of the Indus gorge, 200 miles out of Kargil. Rounding a curve we came in sight of Leh, a bustling bazaar which stretched out at the foot of a maze of buildings rising up to the massive block of the fortified palace of the kings of Ladakh. Here was the long-elusive goal of many a past adventurer, a town only recently opened to foreigners.

Working our way through caravans of yaks and strings of ponies advancing to the tinkle of bells, we stopped in the heart of the bazaar. Here in the clear light of high altitude a crowd of red-robed monks mingled with men and women in fine burgundy homespun gowns. The open smiles of pretty girls with shining braids and abundant necklaces of coral and turquoise reminded me that we were in a world far different from that of Muslim bazaars. Gone were the veiled women and the placid, almost apathetic merchants; here we breathed the gay, carefree atmosphere of Tibet. Portly matrons ushered about surprisingly beautiful daughters with high cheekbones and almond, light brown eyes. Although the general appearance of the population was Mongolian it was easy to see that their blood was mixed with that of some earlier Caucasian stock, a mixture producing particularly fine looking women.

Francke's discovery in Leh of several tombs containing elongated skulls was significant proof that once the area had been inhabited by another race. As soon as we had found lodgings in Leh we set out in quest of these ancient graves, excavated by Francke in 1910. Alas, search as we did in the company of local scholars we were unable to find any traces of the tombs. We presumed that they had been destroyed in the recent development of Leh, today surrounded by a large military camp.

A few miles south of Leh the upper Indus valley opens out to form a broad plain hemmed in by snow peaks. Upon this plain, dominating small villages, rise the vast pyramidal outlines of numerous monasteries. These great Lamaist institutions recall the invasion of the area by Tibetans in the eighth, and later the tenth century. This first invasion was the result of Tibet waking up as a military force in 640 under its great king, Songtsen Gampo. It was he who united what until then had been small divided agricultural communities to establish the great Kingdom of Tibet whose boundaries he extended right across Central Asia to China, and westwards deep into what we knew from the ibex carvings to have been Minaro territory.

In great excitement Nordrop took us to visit one of these monasteries, that of Tikse, whose abbot was his friend. The Tikse monastery, neatly whitewashed with its hive-like cells, colleges, refectories, libraries and storerooms, rose in a majestic cone to support the ochre-coloured assembly halls, a showcase of Himalayan piety. After we had climbed up to his small gilt cell, the abbot bade us sit down on a fine wool carpet. A pious man, he had stopped his monks from selling any of their possessions to tourists and saw to it that his charges observed the strictest rules of the faith. Nordrop, bowing low, presented the abbot with his entire savings in exchange for several holy books. We were then given tea and, later, sacred pills wrapped in holy cloth to protect us on our journey.

The towering palace of the Ladakhi kings in Leh, together with the grandiose monasteries, recalled what had been the ultimate fate of our neolithic forefathers. Over the years the neolithic ibex hunters had become increasingly dependent upon agriculture for survival. Eventually fixed, self-supporting agricultural communities had fallen here, as in the rest of the world, victims of the men whom they had elected as warlords to defend their fields. Gradually this ruling élite came to own and monopolize the land, reducing the farmers to the rank of mere labourers.

As the population slowly increased, the problem arose of how the excess people were to be employed. For the unemployed landless peasants there were few options. They could become soldiers for their overlords and seek fortune, and often death, through plunder and war; or they could emigrate to new lands; their third and last option was, as it had been in feudal Europe, to become monks. Thus the great monasteries that still today dominate the ·skyline all over Ladakh, as they once did in Europe, should be seen not so much as symbols of faith but rather as institutions created to absorb excess population. In Ladakh these monasteries are the sign of an agricultural society rich enough to support a section of its population which is not required to do productive work, yet too poor in land to allow them to marry and have families.

Contrary to what many people think, Himalayan monasteries do not exist by means of charity. They are universities to which second sons are sent by their families, who support them there in the understanding that they do not marry and further burden the limited resources of the land.

Leaving Leh and driving east towards the disputed border with Chinese-occupied Tibet we now headed our jeep for the high pastures, the great Chang-tang, or northern plains, which from Ladakh lead over into central Tibet. These plains today are inhabited by nomadic Tibetan herders. Although we were not allowed by the Indian Army to go right into the northern plains, we nevertheless managed to make an important discovery by interviewing several nomads who established that their high pastures were dotted with ibex carved stones, right up to the Tibetan frontier. What was particularly interesting was that the nomads did not know by whom or for what purpose these stones had been carved. This we believed to indicate that the herders were relative newcomers to the area, a fact supported by Tibetan literary evidence. Before their arrival this region must have been populated by either Minaro or a very closely related white and perhaps Aryan people.

We were prevented from pursuing our research any further east than the Tantak monastery by the soldiers of the numerous military checkpoints. So we turned and made our way back down the Indus past Leh to the monastery at Alchi, famous for its beautiful twelfth-century frescoes. Not far from this monastery, where we set up camp high on the steep banks of the Indus, we found a great abundance of very ancient-looking carved boulders with representations of humans, ibex and strange deer-like animals. These carvings, the most elegant we had seen so far on our journey, had been drawn schematically in a delicate style, the hallmark of Stone Age man's finest art.

Having photographed the more remarkable of our finds we left Alchi to proceed towards Khalatse, site of the strategic bridge across the mighty Indus. As we drove along the ledge of cliffs which fell down to the river I noticed piles of gravel all along our route, as if someone had dug trenches or deep furrows. This was a reminder that we were now in what could have been described as the gold strip of the Indus. Here for centuries man had searched for gold.

Roughly from Alchi down to Khalatse, and beyond into Minaro territory, the banks of the Indus are known to contain gold. It may not be merely coincidence that a few miles upstream from Alchi the Zanskar River joins the Indus, bringing down in its silt-laden waters gold dust from Zanskar, gold dust for which I had panned in Zanskar in 1978. My assistants at that time had been a monk and a local carpenter from the village of Pimo. Standing by the water's edge, for a whole day we had passed sand through a wicker sieve before using a metal dish to sift the finer sand in which we found, for a full day's work, but a few grains of gold. Yet I knew that more professional gold-seekers could have found larger quantities. Strangely enough, today the Zanskaris, like the inhabitants of Ladakh, are not gold mad – in fact panning for gold is considered a lowly, unclean task, one best left to the blacksmiths who are considered to be of inferior lineage. The reason for this reluctance seems to be that in digging for gold one is believed to be tampering with the home of the gods of the soil of the ancient 'religion of men'.

Here in Ladakh the river ran at the bottom of a steep canyon, so that gold-seekers had been obliged to dig up the old deposits stranded in various layers on the deep, high sides of the river gorge. Excitedly we went over to investigate the sites of these excavations. I wondered how the ancient prospectors had managed to locate the gold-bearing sands under tons of gravel and rocks along the river's banks. The German scholar Herrmann believed that it was perhaps just ordinary ants that had shown the miners where to dig. Yet he had placed the land of the gold-digging ants up the Suru River where, in fact, the banks of the river are not steep, and one would not need any sort of a probe to find the gold along the riverside. Herrmann, one must add, had never been to Ladakh and had based his conclusions on the simple fact that until recently gold had still been extracted from the Suru River, while gold digging had long been abandoned along the Indus.

Surely, Missy suggested, we should be able to obtain from the people here details about local gold digging techniques, maybe even legends linking ants to the location of gold. This idea, I knew, had already occurred to Francke, who had painstakingly interviewed the inhabitants of Khalatse, the village towards which we were now headed, for stories concerning ants and gold.

My research had led me to a paper of Francke's entitled 'Two Ant Stories from the Territory of the Ancient Kingdom of Western Tibet, A Contribution to the Question of the Gold Digging Ants'. The two ant stories Francke had unearthed were in fact rather disappointing. One was a tale told to him in Khalatse of how a certain King K'ri-t'ob planned to marry his daughter to a minister, but to his dismay the minister asked that the girl's dowry, composed of household utensils, should all be of pure gold. Consulting with his *wazir* the king learnt that gold lay hidden at the bottom of a nearby lake; a local lama thereupon caused it to rain and several ants came out of the ground. One of these was the King of Ants who, under menace, agreed to extract the gold from the centre of the lake. Wires were then tied around the waists of some two thousand ants, which burrowed down to recover the gold (the wires around the waists, as the story goes, being the origin of the characteristic narrowing of the ants' bodies). With the gold of the lake the king was, in the end, able to marry off his daughter, who of course lived happily ever after.

I was not greatly taken with this tale, so different from the original story of Herodotus which claimed that the ants were bigger than foxes and smaller than dogs, and that these ants brought up not gold but gold-bearing sands. The fact that Francke, and later myself, could find no better stories about gold-digging ants in the area indicated that either the local Drok-pa were not the true Dards of Herodotus, or that the land of the gold-digging ants might be many miles away, perhaps in another land; or lastly that, as nearly everyone believed, the tale was but a myth. Maybe the Himalayan scholar S. S. Gergan was right when after having cross-questioned Baltis, Ladakhis and Minaro over thirty years he concluded in 1977: 'It is not understood how the Greeks and the Romans got these stories.'

I found it hard to accept the story as pure myth, however. There is rarely smoke without fire. And what smoke! Had not the story of the gold-digging ants found its way into Indian, Chinese, Mongolian and Tibetan literature, not to mention the very numerous Greek and Roman references? Yet nor could I accept Dr Herrmann's conclusion, based in part on the story of Francke, that the ants were originally normal ants and that the further one got from the gold-bearing rivers of Ladakh the more the ants grew in size and ferocity until they became, in India, giant red ants which could kill an elephant, and in Greece, bigger than foxes. Whereas, still according to Herrmann, the closer one got to the gold the more the ants diminished in size and ferocity to become normal ants, as in the story recorded by Francke at Khalatse. Dr Herrmann's theory really amounted to declaring the whole giant ant business a legend. On the other hand Ladakh does correspond approximately to the location given by Herodotus, who placed the land of the ants as near as Kaspatyros, the town of Kasyapa, the founder of Kashmir.

Reading and rereading the classics I had asked myself many times, what if Herodotus and the other great writers had spoken the truth? Should we believe that there really were ants bigger than foxes and smaller than dogs? Strabo recounts that Nearchos, like Megasthenes, had seen such ants in the palace of the Persian king and that they had fur 'like that of a panther'. Ants with fur, bigger than foxes! This was certainly a mighty frightening, improbable insect.

Over the centuries it seems that the gold beds of the Indus had lost much of their attraction. No doubt the best beds had been overworked, for no one panned for gold here any longer. Once local farmers had paid tribute to the Ladakhi kings in gold, which was used to adorn the numerous statues housed in the monasteries – objects which were plundered in 1840 by the troops of the Raja of Jammu, whose lieutenant, Zorawara Singh, conquered Ladakh, sending back to Jammu 170 pony-loads of gold and silver. Modern methods may possibly be employed once again to exploit the gold of the Indus, but for the moment the only evidence of this former gold rush were the piles of gravel, dug up and sifted, along either side of the mighty Indus beside which we were now driving in our quest for the elusive origin of the legend of the gold-digging ants.

Carvings near Alchi.

7

THE UNICORN
AND THE FAIRIES

It was late when we reached the bridge which stands at Khalatse. A
military checkpost, barbed wire and a big sign proclaiming
'BEYOND THIS POINT FOREIGNERS NOT ALLOWED'
reminded us that today, as yesterday, as for many thousands of
years, this bridge is the key strategic point of the area. Beyond it,
we knew only too well, began the narrow gorges of the Indus, the
territory of the last surviving Minaro.

A place of such importance is not without a long history. That of
Khalatse was longer than we expected. Our first glimpse of the past
was the ruined walls of what looked like a Scottish castle set upon a
pinnacle of rock. This, we learnt, was the fortress of Na Luk (Black
Sheep), a Minaro warlord who had fought the troops of the Tibetan
king Skilde Nymagon here in the tenth century.

It was already getting dark in the deeply encased valley when we
set about looking for a place to camp. Resourceful as ever, Nordrop
soon latched on to a farmer who agreed to let us pitch our tents in
the field he had just harvested. In no time the man was sitting beside
our tents examining our gear, while I noted his long thin nose and
Minaro looks.

It was not long before I was asking the man if he knew of any tales
about ants or other animals digging up gold. My question was met
with a now familiar blank expression. No, was his reply, he had
never heard of anything like that. The following day similar questions received the same negative response from other villagers.
What did this mean? Could it be that the Minaro after all were not
the original Dards?

To find out we began to record some of the Minaro's early
history. Under the shadow of their ancient castle at Khalatse we

learnt about the bitter struggle that had occupied the Minaro and the Tibetans in the tenth century. Although Black Sheep, the Minaro leader, had been defeated the Tibetans had since left the villages of the Lower Indus alone, which explains why south of Khalatse the Minaro have retained intact their language and most of their customs.

The courage of the early Minaro is still remembered at Khalatse, where we were told how one of the Minaro warriors, seeing that all was lost, called his men into the main hall of his fort. Preferring to die rather than surrender, he had his men knock down the central pillar of the hall so that he and his companions should die together as the building collapsed. Another tale told how further down the Indus at Dah the Tibetans had attempted to press the Minaro into forced labour for the Tibetan king. This they had obstinately re-sisted. Infuriated, the Tibetans latched on to a particular old man and tried to force him to work. When he too stubbornly refused the Tibetans decided to cement him into a wall. Slowly the stones rose up round the old man, burying him alive, but right to the very end the brave Minaro refused to give in.

Ever since this time the Ladakhis have held a grudge against the Minaro, calling them dirty and having disparaging sayings about them. One of these runs, 'As you would not sit under a sword, do not give a Minaro a high place', another, 'Thorns are not wood, sheep lungs are not meat, Minaro are not men.'

Today in Khalatse some old people still speak a few words of Minaro and say certain prayers in Shina because they are not sure that their divinities have learnt Tibetan. The obstinacy of the Min-aro in retaining their language, customs and ancient beliefs is remarkable – all the more so because as the Tibetans pushed on west they enveloped the Minaro villages so that today the Minaro of the Indus are entirely surrounded, as are the Minaro of Zanskar, by Tibetan-speaking Buddhists and Muslims of mixed Mongolian stock. As one Minaro declared to me, talking of his devout Budd-hist and Muslim neighbours, 'God distributed the various faiths in the form of sacred books, but the Minaro, we ate our books so that we have no particular written religious code, but just believe in fairies.'

When I had made friends with the owner of the field in which we were camping I asked him whether he had any *chang*, in thirsty anticipation of finding Tibetan beer. The man's reply came as a surprise.

'*Rash chang* (wine)? I'm afraid I'm out of it.'

'Wine?' I said, bewildered. 'Do you mean that you make wine here?'

Thus it was that I met my first Himalayan wine grower. I now noted that the man had a typical burgundy wine-grower's face with chubby, rosy cheeks.

'Do grapes really grow here?' I asked, still astonished.

'Yes, we have lots, but they are not fully ripe yet.' The next morning he promised to show me how he made his wine.

In Kargil I had heard about wine being made in Garkund, but I did not think I would find it this far east in Khalatse, although I knew that it had once been made further east by several Tibetan and Bhutanese communities. To the west Islam was responsible for the destruction of so many of the vineyards which had once adorned the hillsides of Asia.

The Mongolian invasions had further deprived the area of the nectar of the gods, the vines which, under the Aryans, had once covered the continent. It was not for nothing that Dionysius of Thebes, god of the vine, had been, according to legend, 'reborn in the East' to teach the Indians how to make wine. Alexander had found wine in the town of Nysa, located not far from the Indus, which he believed to have been populated by the sons of the soldiers of Dionysius. As is well known, Alexander had a weakness for wine, but alas, like Himalayan gold, Himalayan wine was not to be his, for on reaching India he made the big mistake of travelling south down the Indus to the Persian Gulf. Had he gone up river he might have reached Minaro territory.

After a breakfast of curry I walked over to our new friend's house, a massive structure of dried earth, bricks and timber. It was already very hot, Khalatse at the bottom of the Indus gorge being heated by the sun like an oven. Less than 10,000 feet above sea level, it is a low point in the western Himalayas and has, as a result, an unusually large amount of apple and apricot trees. These grow around the terraced barley fields. My friend showed me his vines, which did not grow trained on sticks, but wild, as creepers, covering the poplar trees or even the fruit trees.. The grapes were green and as small as those I had found in Kargil.

My friend led me back to his house whose door was appropriately guarded by a stuffed ibex head. Inside I was taken aback by the size of the rooms and the number of shiny pots on shelves beside the hearth. His wife was sitting by the hearth, looking European in spite of her dark red Ladakhi gown with its austere straight collar. She was not in the least bit shy – quite the contrary, as is, I now appreciated, the Minaro style. I was soon being offered Tibetan tea and while secretly deploring that there was no wine left to drink, listened as my host gave a detailed account of how he made wine.

His recipe was simple. He would take the grapes and place them one by one in an earthenware pot which he would then cover with a cloth and seal with damp clay for a day. After this he would pour the resultant juice into another, larger pot which would be left open to ferment for seven days. The wine, having fermented, would be filtered out and transferred into yet another earthenware pot which would be sealed, to be then kept for one or several years! The wine would be a clear, transparent colour at first but would, he assured me, take on an amber hue on maturing. The left-over mush would be kept and mixed with water to produce a second-rate drink called *mayura*.

The recipe surprised me a little because the grapes were not crushed. Later I learned of four different techniques used by the Minaro for making their wine. Some squeezed the grapes, others let them ooze their own juice by piling them on a stone slab. Some let the juice ferment for fifteen days, some filtered the juice before it was fermented, others did not. This variety of techniques I knew to be matched in France, where nearly every wine grower has his own personal method.

Since grapes were a luxury in the Himalayas, wine was not drunk as freely as barley beer, but was reserved for special occasions.

Having finished discussing wine, I went back to the camp where I had an appointment with one of the village elders, a wise man by the name of Chemet. This man, on learning about my interest in carved stones, led me to the fields which dropped down from the village to the Indus. There among the grassy terraces were many boulders, some with ibex drawn over them, others, interestingly, bearing ancient Tibetan inscriptions. Some of these had been written eight hundred years ago by Tibetan soldiers who had been garrisoned at Khalatse, guarding the bridge over the river and collecting taxes on passing goods. I was not able to decipher these inscriptions, but I knew that the oldest and most interesting inscriptions in Ladakh had been found at Khalatse. Some of these were discovered by the Rev. Francke and had been studied by other famous scholars. One inscription, which was too damaged to be read, was in Brahmi characters, a script used in the days of King Ashoka; this inscription was believed to be from the second century BC. Another inscription was of the Kushana period and dated from approximately AD 187; according to Petech it referred to the second great Kushan king, Ubima Kavthisa. This inscription it is now feared has been destroyed, blasted to bits by the engineers who built the new bridge over the Indus in 1907. Later inscriptions written in Tibetan, like the ones I had seen, had been recorded in large numbers. Francke calls them 'royal Tibetan inscriptions', observing that they generally gave the names of soldiers who must have camped here.

Moving further downstream we investigated the banks of the Indus near the ruins of an old bridge and castle. Here we found, as in Alchi, hundreds of stones carved with ibex, and some with horses. To our regret we saw that only recently many stones bearing ibex carvings and inscriptions had been smashed with sledge hammers or blasted to provide rocks for the new military road.

Rummaging around looking for stones, shouting out to each other whenever we made an exceptional find, we soon attracted the attention of the soldiers who guarded the bridge. I was forced to give lengthy explanations as to why we were overturning stones and taking 'suspicious' photographs left and right. They eventually calmed down when I produced a letter from Sheikh Abdullah requesting that we be given 'all needed assistance in Kashmir'. In the meantime, around the checkpost, Missy had found yet more carved rocks. Soon the soldiers themselves got caught by rock fever and started to help us in our search.

Leaving the bridge at length, we retraced our steps for two miles up river to the ancient fortress of Ba-lu Khar, a natural rock

pyramid rising right out of the Indus, carved with step-like plat-
forms and levelled at the top. Just below the summit is the mouth of
a great cave closed in with blocks of stone. The story goes that this
was once a Minaro fortress, later transformed by the Tibetans into a
customs house where taxes were levied on the great trade route.

Sitting beside the massive bulk of Ba-lu Khar I reflected that
however many political regimes had come and gone, fighting for
control of this strategic place, little here had really changed. The
farmers of Khalatse, in spite of having been conquered, were little
different from the earlier Minaro settlers, retaining the traditions of
wine making and even ibex hunting, traditions stretching back to
the far mists of antiquity. There was now little doubt in my own
mind, although we had yet to prove it, that the Minaro had lived
here in the days of Herodotus.

As the sun disappeared behind the steep cliffs bordering the
Indus, a cold wind swept up the mighty river making the roaring
waters glisten steel-grey in the twilight. How insignificant in the
face of nature seem human political endeavours, the agitations of a
species driven by a strong instinct for survival and the contrary
follies of an unpredictable imagination. Certainly homo sapiens is
all too often irrational. Yet it is, alas, in these 'follies of the mind'
that we are unique. As the Tibetans say; 'Donkeys do not drink
beer,' or talk politics and act out magic rituals to invisible spirits
said to inhabit the sky, the mountain tops or the bowels of the earth
– fantasies for which so many of us have been prepared to die.

Innumerable wars have been waged in the name of religion. Did
the ibex hunter have a saner creed, I wondered.

This we now hoped to find out as, the following morning, we left
the depths of the Indus gorge and drove back towards Kargil, keen
to get news of our request for the permit to proceed into Minaro
territory.

Climbing out of the gorge above Khalatse, up nineteen hairpin
curves, we entered what seemed like a tormented white sandpile of
eroded cliffs and jagged sugarloaf mounds of mineral. On one of
these stood the great monastery of Lamayuru, a huge complex of
whitewashed buildings crowned by a massive, six-storey assembly
hall whose elegant sloping walls proclaim the sober talent of Hima-

layan architects. Here, thousands of miles from Lhasa, stands a group of buildings which would not shame the Tibetan capital. As we approached by jeep, monks came out to greet us. They belonged to the little known Kadampa sect, one of the seventeen sects of Tibetan Lamaism. I was interested to note that the monastery and the adjoining village were entirely built upon a hive of caves, caves similar to those I had found in Mustang.

Pacing through the gilt halls of the numerous chapels, with their fierce-looking divinities surrounding placid, smiling images of Buddha, Nordrop and I searched for the most erudite of the local monks. In the end we located a middle-aged monk who seemed to have a literate grasp of his religion. To our surprise this monk, like others we interviewed, stated that the monastery had originally been an entirely Drok-pa (Minaro) institution and that this area had originally been Minaro territory.

'How do you know this?' I queried.

'We have heard it from generation to generation,' the monk replied.

He then told me that a few of the monks actually came from Minaro villages and that the Minaro were held in high esteem by the monks. Here, once a year, a great festival was held, to which Minaro in their hundreds came from their villages along the Indus.

I was interested to learn that the Lamayuru monastery, along with those of Lingshit and Rangdum, and the villages near them, formed a sort of independent monastic republic, free from the control of the kings of Ladakh and Zanskar. It seemed that they had originally served the local herders and nomads, no doubt the Minaro of old who came there to pray and might once have inhabited the local caves in winter.

On our way to Kargil from the Lamayuru monastery we passed through Henescu, Kharbu and the Mulbekh region which according to stories and legends may have been the heart of ancient Minaro territory. Certainly today the men, especially those from Kharbu and Chitgan, have dominantly Minaro features – slim noses, thin pointed faces and elongated skulls. The river that runs through Mulbekh is known as the Waka, *wa* (or *ua*) meaning water in Minaro, another clear indication that the area had once been Minaro territory.

At Mulbekh, beside the gigantic statue of the 'Buddha to Come', near which I had first seen Minaro in 1975, we came upon a whole party of Minaro returning to their villages along the Indus. The women all wore strange, sock-like bonnets folded flat across their heads supporting bouquets of faded flowers. On their breasts glistened saucer-like copper mirrors which shone in the evening sun. I tried to talk them into posing for my camera but was greeted with loud and intimidating protests. It was all too easy, it seemed, to provoke the anger of these Amazons. The young girls I again found extremely beautiful, with their long plaited hair and pale skin. Their mothers on the other hand were a bunch of noisy hags. Their faces were uncannily familiar, the scowling faces of angry European women of the most aggressive kind. It took no great stretch of the imagination to see them in another costume, living in the West. To many I could have assigned the names of women back home.

Back in Kargil, still finding no news of our permits, we resolved to return to Zanskar. As we prepared for this journey I carried on my interviews with Minaro in the bazaar, where to my great pleasure I once again ran into my friend Dorje Namgyal, still followed closely by his little boy. From him and other Minaro I now obtained detailed confirmation that the inhabitants of the Kingdom of Women were truly ruled by their ladies. Polyandry, a custom by which women can have several husbands, was much practised in their villages. Most women would sleep with, and if they wished marry all the men in their first husband's household. Thus if there were three brothers in a home they would all marry and have children with the same wife. This practice, known as fraternal polyandry, extended also to any other man who might happen to live under the same roof on a permanent or even a temporary basis.

There is reason to believe that this custom was once common over most of Central Asia and Tibet – the very custom that the early Emperors of China so despised and fought to have abolished. Polyandry is still practised today in about one family in ten, in Tibet, Ladakh and Zanskar, but in the Minaro settlements, I now learnt, the proportion is very much higher. Six to eight married women out of ten still have more than one husband, the true sign of a matriarchal regime.

To conclude from this fact that the Minaro were the famed Eastern

Amazons first mentioned by Herodotus is a long step which I shall not take. But it is possible that rumours might have reached the West to the effect that in Central Asia women had several husbands and ruled the household; from there it is not hard to imagine them riding horses and shooting arrows, as brave as, if not braver than their men.

Meanwhile I was discovering from Dorje Namgyal and my other informants that married life for the Minaro was not much of a dream. Their women, many complained, ruled their lives and were generally considered unmanageable. With several husbands, they had little trouble running the house by playing one husband against another.

'How do you know who is the true father of a child in your family?' I asked Dorje, who shared his wife with a cousin.

'One has to ask the mother,' came the startling reply. This is at variance with the Tibetan custom that generally considers children to be of the oldest husband.

The matriarchal aspect of Minaro society is reflected in their religious beliefs, for no male gods are to be found in their heavens. This now became clear as we studied in further detail the Minaro's archaic religion. Their two main divinities are Gyantse-Lhamo and Shiringmen-Lhamo, the fairy goddesses of fortune and chance and of fertility respectively. Both are women. Alongside these two main divinities are other local female divinities specific to each village. In Garkund for example they have Kushu-lo-Lhamo and Zangmanden-Lhamo, the first the goddess of weather, the second the protectress of the village and of hunters; both goddesses are considered to be young and beautiful fairies, queens of the lesser fairies to be exact. The main goddess, Gyantse-Lhamo in Tibetan, is actually called Mun-Gyantse in Minaro, meaning 'all-embracing' fairy. She resides, as does the Minaro Babalachen in Zanskar, on the top of a mountain.

The basis of Minaro belief, I now gathered, is that happiness is equated with abundance and fertility, both of which are dispensed by the principal goddesses. From this one sees that the Minaro religion is a very simple one, having certain traits in common with the early pagan beliefs of the Greeks – a cult of Mother Nature, ruler of the elements, the land and its bounties.

To be pleasing to the goddesses both men and women must be

ritually clean. This cleanliness is achieved by respecting certain taboos; neither touching a cow nor eating its products; not touching the plates or utensils of impure persons such as pregnant women, young mothers until a month after giving birth, women having their periods, and people who have just had sexual intercourse. Thorough cleansing is brought about not only through the sacred properties of juniper smoke but also by appropriate good behaviour. This concern with ritual purity is a typically Aryan trait, very apparent in the conduct of the Brahmins, the high caste Aryan priests of Hinduism, while on the other hand the Minaro's repulsion to cows, the Aryan's most sacred animal, speaks of a possibly earlier origin.

Between the goddesses and man stands a whole legion of lesser fairies who live in trees, near springs, or in the mountains guarding the flocks of ibex who are ruled, as has been seen, by a one-horned ibex ram. It is interesting to note that on many old tapestries in Europe unicorns are often shown with a beard, not unlike that of an ibex ram. Indeed unicorns often resemble ibex which, being very tall, may easily be confused with ponies. Perhaps it was not too fanciful to suppose that one-horned ibex were at the root of our Western myths about unicorns.

From Dorje Namgyal I learnt how fairies can be very dangerous if angered. If a man meets a fairy she may follow him back to his house and cause disease, or even death. One recognizes a fairy by her feet, which are turned inward. It is rumoured that some ordinary women are in fact fairies. At night they remove the main beam of the house, replacing it with a long hair from their head, then they fly away on the beam, much as our own witches fly around on broomsticks.

Through this talk of fairies I obtained more details about the Minaro's methods of hunting. In order to secure ibex the hunter needs the help of the fairy goddesses of good fortune and abundance. If he is ritually clean and pleasing to the fairies, they will aid the hunter in shooting an ibex by sitting on his shoulder. If the ibex being stalked kneels the hunter must not shoot, as this is a sign that it is under the special protection of the fairies. On their return successful hunters must offer the intestines and the heart of their prey to Gyantse-Lhamo in gratitude, along with the horns. After that the hunter offers up to the divinity a carved image of the ibex he has killed. These are not to be carved anywhere but, as I now at long last found out, in a 'sheltered hollow or vale at the foot of a cliff which is facing the mountain where the goddess resides'. The complex directions, confirmed by several people, explained to us why until now we had not exactly understood where to look for ibex carvings.

It seems that by offering the ram's horns to the goddess the 'guilt' of killing the fairies' animals is cancelled out, while the carving of an ibex restores the dead animal to life. Thus ibex horns and the drawn images of ibex are simply offerings made to the female divinities in gratitude and exchange for the animal's life. I was now certain that the ibex were not considered gods by the Minaro, as many scholars believed; the rock carvings were made solely as symbolic retribution.

The simple logic behind this exchange could well be the best explanation for some of the hunting scenes found on the walls of ancient caves in Europe, be they images of ibex or bison. Bearing in mind how the Minaro recalled the days before they had bows and arrows, it seemed beyond doubt that they were either directly descended from or closely related to the earliest Himalayan inhabitants: an Indo-European speaking people of Caucasian blood, a people who, like the ancient Scythians, never washed, and who like them, and also many Western people including the Celts, considered juniper smoke to be a purifying element, and goats to be the most worthy sacrifice to their gods.

As I began to study in detail the ordinance of the Minaro festivals, their marriage rites and other rituals, my discoveries led me every day to consolidate further my conviction that here was a strangely unique people. Thus I learnt how, on New Year's day (the winter solstice), two boys are dressed in goatskins to take upon themselves the evil of the village before being chased away at sundown. Similarly, whenever an epidemic strikes a village a young black goat is taken round all the houses and then driven out in the belief that it will take with it the disease. That all such beliefs have a familiar ring to us western Indo-Europeans is understandable since they may have reached Europe through the eastern Scythians, the Saca, one-time neighbours of the Minaro. The Minaro's dress, a short jacket cut high above the knees and narrow trousers, both ornamented with geometric designs, recalled the exact clothes worn by Scythians from north of the Black Sea as depicted on a vessel found in a Scythian tomb at Kuloba.

One elaborate ritual which underlines the importance of the horse in Minaro culture seemed to confirm definite links between the Minaro and the ancient horse-riding Scythians who, in the wake of the early Aryans, spread all over Central Asia in the sixth century BC. The festival, called 'the payment of a horse', is still held in all the Minaro settlements, in Zanskar and on the Indus, on the first day of the second month of the Tibetan agricultural calendar. On that day men are not to wear shoes or even to mention them, while donkeys are not supposed to bray. At dawn in each household a feast is prepared of 'clean' foods: goat or sheep meat, goats' milk, fried peas and cakes. This food, together with some jewellery, is presented to select horses by barefoot men; the food is also offered to the household dog, dogs being considered pure by the Minaro, no doubt because of their vital role in the chasing of ibex. A chosen horse, preferably white, is marked along its back, over its shoulders and rump with red clay and then offered to Babalachen or Gyantse-Lhamo, while incense is passed over its body. Once presented to the goddess the horse is never to be ridden again (although if a family is particularly poor the horse may be ridden, but not for a full week after the ceremony). Such an offering is considered to bring about rain and a good harvest. In Gyagam the people claim that the perspiration of a horse symbolizes rain. When they offer up a horse to their goddesses they sometimes, as a variant, drape the horse in white cloth. The horse then becomes sacred property and is set free. The skulls of dead horses are buried near houses to keep away evil, a custom which is also encountered in Europe.

The favourite game of the Minaro is none other than polo. Minaro polo has nothing to do with the Afghan game, which is played with the carcass of a goat, but is very much the same game as played in Europe now and in Iran 2,500 years ago.

There are polo fields in all the Minaro villages of the Indus. The Minaro claim that the game was invented by the semi-mythical king, the Lion of Gil (Gilgit), who founded their earliest settlements. The game is played with a 'baton' (stick) on a narrow field some 280–300 paces long by only 45–50 paces wide, generally bordered by a stone wall or embankment. There are 4 to 6 players a side. The ball is made from the root of the juniper tree and must be large enough not to penetrate the socket of the player's eye. The sticks are of birch and the mallet head is horn-shaped. Stones placed on the ground represent the goal, and a goal can only be counted if the rider dismounts and touches the ball to the ground behind the goal stones.

Although 'polo' is the archaic pronunciation of the Tibetan word for ball, the game may have been introduced to the Minaro by the Persians who partially controlled in the fith century BC what was once Minaro territory: Gilgit, Skardo and perhaps the present Minaro villages along the Indus. The game was later adopted by the Tibetan soldiers who were garrisoned in the area in the eighth century, and more recently by the Muslim rulers of Skardo who became very keen on the game. The British took up polo after seeing it played by Shins in the Gilgit area. Of all the various horse games with a ball the western Himalayan form of polo is the closest to the modern game. Perhaps it is not too far-fetched to suppose that the Persians had actually learnt the game from the early Minaro.

The many traits which, like their language, linked the Minaro to either ancient Iran or the early Scythians raised the question of whether they might themselves have emigrated from Central Asia at an early date. For several reasons I did not believe this. I had begun to suspect that they had probably acquired their language and many other customs only from their contact with the ancient Persian Empire which, in the fifth century BC, had ruled great tracts of western India and the Himalayas along the Indus. The Persians had, after all, extended their rule to the east for a much longer time than the rapid conquest of western India by Alexander. It was therefore natural that they should have left their mark on the Minaro.

Throughout my quest as to the origins of the Minaro I had to fight that traditional Western tendency, mocked by Clark, of wanting to see every people linked to those of our own antiquity, be they Greek or Persian. Modern biologists and physical anthropologists, thanks to the study of blood groups, have shown the remarkable staying power of ancient people. This makes it quite probable that the Minaro, like the Kailash and other fair tribes of Asia, had not migrated there in recent times, but had populated the region long before those relatively recent classical invasions of the Aryans and Scythians – invasions which, all told, probably had a greater cultural impact than a genetic one. After all, our recorded history stretches back barely 2,500 years, whereas man has populated the globe for over 100,000. It would be quite justifiable to believe that the Minaro had acquired over that time several different languages and customs from many different cultures while retaining some of their earliest traditions and original genetic traits. I was becoming increasingly convinced that they could very well be not just ancient Aryans but proto-Aryans.

To shed more light on the subject, and having received no news of our permits, we now prepared to set out on a long journey right across Zanskar. For not only did we have a rendezvous with our friends the Minaro of Gyagam, who have retained perhaps more than those of the Indus the traditions of our past, but we planned also to enter the highest of all Himalayan regions, the great plains of Rupchu. In this region live today the westernmost primitive nomads of Tibet, the spearhead of that mighty invasion which no doubt had chased the Minaro out of Central Asia and Tibet.

8

POISONED ARROWS

Helped by Mr Kakpori and Nordrop, Missy bought stores and provisions for the rugged two hundred mile journey on foot and pony to the 15,000 foot plateau of Rupchu. This region, rarely visited by foreigners, the very highest portion of the Himalayan tableland, is the true roof of the world.

Leaving Kargil we sped up the Suru valley, leaving the road to examine a rarely visited gigantic rock image of Chamba, 28 feet tall, on which we discovered an ancient yet unrecorded Tibetan inscription that we were unable to decipher. Then we drove on over the Pensi-la pass, reaching Gyagam in the evening where we were greeted by Tsewan, the local village priest. Bidding goodbye to our jeep driver we entered once again a world in which travel is set by the pace of one's heart, the rhythm of one's feet upon those small trails that were once the only web to link mankind.

Once we had set up camp, Nordrop and I went to Tsewan's house. Bending low we fumbled around in the dark, groping our way up the stone stairs from the ground floor stables to a sunlit, enclosed patio on the first floor. Here in summer Tsewan, his wife, children and old parents lived around a smoky, yak-dung fire; sleeping under the stars, enjoying the few months of sunlight and fresh air, knowing that soon they would have to seek refuge from the long, cold winter in the dark underground living-room below.

Looking at Tsewan's old father, whose face resembled that of a Greek shepherd's, I noted from his dress that the Minaro of Zanskar were already well advanced in the process of Tibetanization, a process I very much wanted to study as this would teach us a great deal about Tibet's own past and its mysterious 'religion of men'. We already knew that the chief Minaro goddess, Gyantse-Lhamo,

91

had been renamed Babalachen (Father Big God) and had acquired all the attributes of the female Minaro divinity, somewhat as Juno replaced the goddess Hera in Greek legend. It was all part of a men's liberation movement in rebellion against the rule of women in neolithic times, when women ruled not only the household but the heavens as well.

By now I was persuaded that the religion of the Minaro was the forerunner of the 'religion of men' of Tibet. Did not both include divinities living on mountain tops who were the 'owners' of the physical world? Both the Tibetans and the Minaro alike erected shrines to these divinities on which they placed rams' horns and juniper branches. It now seemed likely that once this cult had been the same, and that originally the early inhabitants of Tibet had believed not in a male mountain god but in a female divinity, owner of the land, a goddess of nature. The changeover had happened in the past in Tibet just as it had recently in Gyagam, where Baba-lachen, the great mountain god, had taken over from the all-encompassing goddess Gyantse-Lhamo.

The survival of the 'religion of men' as a belief in Tibet parallel to Buddhism could therefore simply be the survival of the ancient nature cult of the early Minaro, a cult which had spread to Tibet in neolithic times when great parts of Tibet, as I now believed, must have been inhabited by a Caucasian people who had built the monuments found by Roerich. In Tibet this ancient religion had been taken over by Bon priests who only later in the twelfth century adopted certain aspects of Buddhism, to the extent that the Bon-po have built monasteries and now wear Buddhist, monk-like gowns. Yet under this Buddhist veneer they still maintain the old beliefs concerning the sacrifice of horses and goats to Mother Nature. There was no doubt in my mind that in the Minaro I had encountered one of the oldest surviving religions of our planet, one here in Gyagam still very much alive.

A key question now in my mind was to find out how similar the Minaro beliefs might be to some of the very ancient pre-Aryan neolithic cults of Europe. Were they linked to those people who had erected our own standing stones? Ever since I had read about and seen the menhirs and dolmens which stretched from Stonehenge to China I had wondered if they were not manifestations of a common creed. 'What was the purpose of these stones?' I naïvely asked the Minaro. I soon came to learn that they differentiated between three types of sacred stones. The first were vertical stones called *Nymatheor* (sun markers), placed to mark the seasons. The villagers of Gyagam showed me six such standing stones silhouetted on a ridge to the east of the village. These stones, they explained, were erected to indicate the solstices, equinox and other events of the solar year. This in itself was fascinating, I thought, recalling how many prehistorians had speculated that our Western menhirs served as calendars.

'Do you build stone tables?' I asked, drawing and describing dolmens, those altar-like arrangements of stones found all over Europe and in parts of Asia.

'Oh, those we call *do-mandal*. They are erected at the foot of mountains, as altars to the mountain god. They were made with three stone legs, sometimes on two levels, like two tripods, one on top of the other.'

One large dolmen near Dah I was told was considered to be the throne of the goddess Gyantse-Lhamo.

As for very large standing stones, these they believed to be the flints of the gods, stone strikers for making fire. Most Himalayans still make fire by striking steel against a stone. Both fire and the sun are held in reverence, as is shown by the role of fire in their New Year celebrations. At this time they paint the sun on the walls of their houses, and all women wear around their necks a *gourre*, or fire disc, a shiny sun-like copper mirror (*gourre* is the Minaro word for fire). These are more than mere ornaments, and are similar to copper or bronze discs associated with fire worship found frequently in neolithic tombs all over Europe and in Asia.

In opposition to the sun and fire, water is also held sacred as symbolic of life. Thus the shrines of Shiringmen-Lhamo, the goddess of fertility, are generally placed beside a spring or rivulet and, whenever possible, near a juniper tree, also a symbol of life. Once a year the Minaro hold a festival of water. At daybreak on the first day of the second lunar month, when the stars are still visible, a young man whose parents must still be alive goes down to the stream or spring barefoot and collects a bowl of water. This is taken into the house and purified over juniper smoke. Then, with a juniper twig, the water is sprayed in offering to the two principal divinities, after which the members of the household wash – probably the only time in the year that they do so. Only then can they wear their goathide shoes again.

Juniper plays a significant role in many of these rituals, not only for the purifying effects of its fragrant smoke but also as a symbol of life. If a man cuts a juniper it is believed that he will die. In Gilgit the Shins, who are related to the Minaro, are known to hold a ceremony in which young women are thrown handfuls of juniper twigs, those who catch them being assured of having children.

Several scholars, among them the linguist Lt. Col. D. L. R. Lorimer, Professor Karl Jettmar and the French linguist G. Fussman, have studied the language and customs of the Shins of Gilgit, Astor, Chilas, Gurres (or Gourais) and other valleys along the upper Indus in Pakistan whose inhabitants, although Muslim, retain here and there a few beliefs which undoubtedly link them with the Minaro. Professor Jettmar was among the first to speculate that behind the fragments of archaic superstition that he was able to record might lie traditions which, by their neolithic nature, could connect the Shins with an archaic proto-Aryan people. Alas, the force of Islam in wiping out previous religious practices has made the study of ancient beliefs of the Shins difficult, if not impossible – a study further frustrated by the slow invasion of the Shins' territory over the years by Pathans from the south and other foreign peoples.

Yet here I should like to pay homage to Professor Jettmar's work and foresight. In one of his books he admonished us that 'it is urgently necessary to start intense field work immediately, in order to save as many traces as possible of the Dards' [Shins'] roots in a pre-Indo-European koine'. Unfortunately the Indian government had so far not been amenable to such wishes, no anthropologist having been allowed to carry out research in the Minaro's forbidden territory. It was thus a real boon to have discovered in Zanskar a large colony which I was free to study at will, awaiting what I hoped would be the privilege of making the first detailed study of the Minaro villages of the Indus.

In the meantime, sitting in the company of Nordrop and Tsewan, the hereditary priests of the Minaro creed, I felt like some reporter parachuted into another planet. Forgotten were the values of that modern world I had, it seemed, abandoned years ago. It was hard to imagine that I had ever lived in Paris, New York, London and Boston, or known of other fires than those of brushwood and sheep droppings whose red glow illuminated the faces of my friends. Tsewan, adjusting his strange hat, spoke as a voice from the past about the overpowering forces of nature to which not only he, but also I myself belonged. No longer were my questions dictated by that cold, morbid scientific curiosity dear to Western scholars; now they came from my heart. I wanted more than anything to gain a better understanding of our relationship with the world around us, of the strange forces that brought about the changing seasons, the migration of birds, life and death. Little did it matter that I knew about modern meteorology and atmospheric pressures; rain and sunshine were, as Tsewan and our own scientists agreed, regulated by the sun, the sun whose course is set in turn by the mysterious attraction of elusive galaxies. Was our knowledge of these forces truly more advanced than Tsewan's? Was science the right route to take in order to trace one's way back to nature?

In the village of Gyagam the pressures of life were few compared to our complex and often distressing modern world. The sun, with its regularity, would point its rays over the adjacent hill, home of the local god, and signal the feast of rejoicing, of giving thanks for the ibex, the grain, the beer and wine; all the bounties of nature. Life was seen as an exchange between the goddesses and man, a relationship that did not call for costly temples, high priests or prophets. The Minaro had no kings or politicians, no nation or empire to legislate their lives beyond the rhythm of the seasons.

The Minaro have been fortunate in preserving a social system based on small village units, in contrast to the vast political entities that elsewhere rule from dawn to dusk over men's lives. I was struck by the lack of hierarchy in their villages. Was this lack of leadership a weakness or, in fact, a strength? It was obvious that the individual castles of the Minaro villages spoke of fragmented power rather than unity.

There is historical evidence to show that Tibet, and maybe much of the world, was once likewise covered with small independent communities. Documents from Tuenhouang attest that in Tibet in ancient times (before the sixth century) 'there was no distinction between the people and their sovereigns'. Another text explains further, 'There were forts on every hill, on every steep rock . . . in those days nobody was able to win out a quarrel, the amount of soldiers was small.' Such is the organization of the Minaro to this day: a people without leaders, without kings, who are all the more ferociously independent for that; a people in fact without a true name, for only a few villagers actually call themselves 'Minaro'.

It is this very individualism – a virtue, I believe – that has allowed the Minaro to survive the onslaught of Tibetan and Islamic forces. Having resisted, it appears, the advance of Alexander in Swat, they were still fighting along the Indus over two thousand years later, this time the British, who never fully subdued the Shina-speaking people of the Chilas area of India's north-west frontier.

Living in Gyagam, in close contact with the Minaro, I could not help but wonder how much their life today differed from that of their earliest forefathers. Had new technology, such as the use of bronze, copper and iron, been matched by a radical new outlook on life, or were they really very much the same as they had always been?

Any reply must be speculative. Yet in trying to answer this question I began to appreciate that, all told, the tools and technology man has bear less upon his life, his behaviour and feelings than do his religious or political ideals. For example, I believe that a Christian and a Muslim living within a similar technological environment are further apart than, say, a rich and poor Christian. Ideals and ideas, it seems, are more decisive in shaping our lives than technology and all that we call progress. On this premiss one must assume that the Minaro's ancestors lived, acted and thought in very much the same manner as their modern descendants. It is really only we, obsessed as we are by technology, who consider the words stone, bronze or steel important in qualifying early man.

In many respects the present-day Minaro, compared to modern man, are to be envied, for their religion is not an oppressive, absolute or intolerant creed. On the contrary their numerous fairies, some good, others malicious, are very similar to the all too human gods of the Greeks: figures of hope and joy, and even of fun, rather than fearful law givers and chastisers. Their life, it seems, is free from political and religious tyranny. Likewise must have lived Stone Age man, whose wit and intelligence, we have reason to believe, was neither more nor less than our own.

As for the Minaro's acceptance of technology, they have come to include a few modern objects of bronze and steel, as employed in Tibet. But in their kitchens I noticed stone pots carved out of black rock and hailing from Minaro settlements north of the Indus. 'They make a far better soup than copper pots,' I was told by all. So much for progress.

Pursuing our investigation into that obscure world of our past we made several interesting discoveries about how the Minaro dispose of their dead. Normally Himalayan Buddhists do not bury their dead but either cremate them, or chop them up and feed them to the vultures, or throw them into rivers. The Minaro, on the other hand, until a few generations ago used to bury their dead, and still do so on occasions. The body, it was explained to me, was set with the legs drawn up (in the foetal position) on its right side, the hands being joined flat as in prayer and tucked under the right cheek. They were buried either in tombs bordered with stones or in a cave, sealed with stone. A small cup of water, a bow and arrows or a gun, jewels and clothes were placed beside the body. Women were buried in the same way as men, but children were simply buried with four rough stones laid in a rectangle around the body.

This was of great interest because such tombs recall in detail the more simple Scythian and other older tombs of Central Asia and the Russian Steppes. Also, in neolithic tombs bodies had often been found in foetal positions. Had any archaeologists, I wondered, noticed that the hands of the ancient skeletons were joined under the right cheek?

During our time in Gyagam we were rewarded with countless details about a world long believed to have totally disappeared, when Europe and Central Asia had suffered the turmoils of conquest and the migrations of the Mongol hordes, followed by the modern ravages of so-called civilization, leaving only tombs and a few standing stones to speak for our ancestors. Now I came to believe that my wild guess had been correct, that the Himalayas were truly the last refuge of our forefathers, and if not the cradle

97

of the Western world, certainly the last stronghold of its early beliefs.

Tsewan showed us how the ritual sacrifices to the gods of the land were performed. In awe we watched as a goat was adorned with red clay and slaughtered before the altar of the ruler of nature, the goat's throat being cut in a ritual that recalled the sacrifice of Abraham, for here too the gods had stopped men from offering up their sons. Children were no longer sacrificed as the supreme offering of man to his divinity, but were replaced by the goat. Later we saw and photographed Tsewan, hands joined in prayer, before a small ibex made of dough he had placed into the cleft of a rock that stood beside the sacred wood. Here in the cleft rock he saw, like our forefathers, a sacred spot that joined heaven and earth.

Another day Tsewan led us far out of the village to a large boulder covered with ibex carvings. This, he told us, was the sacred altar which marked the territorial limits separating the village of Gyagam from that of Hameling. The stone was known as Basardik in Minaro, and Latho Phobrang in Tibetan. It marked not only the boundaries between the two villages but the crossroads of two trails, one leading to the ford across the main river, the other coming down from the Pensi-la pass. By all accounts this was a very sacred place. At the altar goats were offered up on the tenth day of the second month in a plea for good crops. A goat was also sacrificed here when there was a marriage between people of the two villages. On this occasion the goat was killed by a young bachelor whose parents had still to be alive. During the sacrifice, the young man would hold in his teeth a juniper branch, symbol of life, until the animal had expired. The blood of the goat was then sprinkled over both the stone and the couple. This was all the more interesting since we had frequently wondered what purpose was served by similar large stones covered with drawings which we had found in remote uninhabitable places, as in Ladakh. We now took them to be primarily territorial markers, serving also as altars for special sacrifices on the occasion of marriages between members of adjoining communities.

Like so many other ibex-carved stones, this one had been super-imposed with Buddhist symbols, possibly to antagonize the Minaro, or maybe simply to increase its holiness. Among other inscriptions was written '*Ki-ki so-so*', a war-cry generally uttered upon crossing a high pass. This cry is shouted along with the invocation '*Lha gyalo*' (The gods are victorious), which was also inscribed on the stone in a rough hand, covering some of the ibex.

Towards the last days of our stay in Gyagam, when I was beginning to think we had uncovered all there was to find, the keeper of the little Buddhist chapel near our camp showed me a bunch of dried flowers which he kept in the chapel.

'*Karé ré?*' I asked, curious as to what they were.

'*Dui mentock,*' he replied. 'Poisonous flowers.'

Rather recklessly I grabbed a few to examine them. They were a deep blue colour, speckled with grains of white; off a single stem grew a dozen or so little hooded flowers. The dried roots of these flowers were deadly, I was told. 'We use them to poison arrows for shooting ibex.'

I had with me a book on medicinal plants and in no time I identified the flower as *Aconitum napellus*, also known as monkshood or wolf's bane. In my book it was described as 'one of the most poisonous plants in our flora'. In medicinal doses, the book continued, 'it acts on the nervous system.' The Aconitum family being very large (there are over seventeen varieties), I did not know for sure what type this was, yet as I heard about its lethal effects I began to appreciate that it was as deadly as curare. Riding a horse at full gallop and shooting a deadly poisoned arrow, the Minaro had beyond doubt once been a force to be reckoned with.

I carefully wrapped a specimen of the dry plant to take home, but soon found dozens growing by the little irrigation channel of the fields. Later I found aconite everywhere in alarming quantities; in fact whole pastures of them could be seen near the monastery of Rangdum (the plant appears to grow best at altitudes above 12,000 feet). Was it a mere coincidence, I wondered, that the strange Caucasian-looking Ainus, a people of great antiquity inhabiting the Hokkaido and Sakhalin islands off the north-west coast of Japan, used aconite to poison the arrows with which they hunted bear and Sikha deer. This is the only recorded use of aconite on arrow heads in the East, other than its presumed use in Bhutan and by the Minaro in Ladakh. On the other hand aconite is common in Europe and might well have been used there once, not only

to poison relatives (a common medieval practice) but also to hunt
game.

A few days before we left Gyagam we were invited by the
villagers to an archery contest that marked the end of the harvest.
The nearby peak above the village, home of Babalachen, echoed
with the sound of drums as one by one the villagers shot their
arrows at an upright wooden plank. It was hardly a grandiose
occasion; the arrows were not poisonous and all but one of the bows
were made of wood. This one, however, was an amazing work of
art, fashioned from laminated slivers of ibex horn glued to a backing of ibex sinew to form a compact, elastic, fibrous mass. A short
bow made for shooting from horseback, it had two 'S' curves
bulging out from the straight handle section – an exact replica of
what is known as the Scythian bow.

The following day Missy, Nordrop and I bade goodbye to our
friends, and having secured horses set out on our journey across
Zanskar to the border of the Rupchu plains populated by Tibetan
nomads. Rupchu is the western extremity of the terrible 14,000 foot
high plateau that extends practically uninterrupted for 2,000 miles
across Tibet to the Great Wall of China.

Everywhere on our way we came across ibex carved rocks and
boundary altars, as well as standing stones. Now of course we
knew exactly where to look, 'in sheltered vales at the foot of cliffs
facing snowpeaks', and 'near crossroads between villages'. On each
fan-like plain that fell into the Zanskar valley we encountered ibex
graffiti and long-abandoned altars to the goddess of nature.

Our journey took us first to Karsha, the monastery where Nordrop had lived from the age of 13. Seen from afar it appeared as a
tapestry hanging from great rust-coloured cliffs upon which were
depicted dozens of small monks' cells that fell like a cascade from
the uppermost assembly halls. Here we collected a large cloth bag
of *tsampa* for Nordrop for the journey east. Nordrop's brother, also
a monk, had brewed for me yet more of his excellent barley
whiskey in a still in the minute adobe cell in which he had spent so
many of his days meditating on the impermanence of life. Truth,
perfection and the absolute, as he and Nordrop believed, lie beyond
our life on earth and can only be achieved with the extinction of our

mortal bodies and their frail senses through which we can never fully perceive them.

Perhaps more endearing than the tenets of this rather nihilistic creed, that gives in theory so little importance to life on earth, is its surprising great tolerance and love for all mankind and living creatures. The Chief Steward of the monastery showed us the spot above the main assembly hall where, in winter, ibex came down in search of food which the monks put out for them.

'Ibex, you know,' he explained, 'are quite tame. They know we will not harm them and so they eat out of our hands.'

I now began to gather more data on the Capra ibex, known in Europe as the Steinbok or Bouquetin. In the Alps they are found at an even greater height than that reached by the chamois. The Asian variety, *Capra siberica*, is larger than its European counterpart and is today found in a territory which extends from Afghanistan to Siberia. On occasions its horns may measure fully 60 inches long. Ibex are also found in Arabia, the Caucasus and Nubia; a breed that spans three continents.

Although sometimes tame, ibex are difficult to hunt. Herds of between 10 and 15 animals always have one of their kind on guard. This animal sits on its hind legs rather like a dog, constantly keeping watch, and in case of danger lets out a sort of whistling sound or a deep grunt.

I very much hoped to see some ibex on our journey, although I knew this might prove difficult as in summer ibex climb up to the snow line, which in the Zanskar range is the highest in the world rising up to 19,000 feet. It is in such remote high areas that the rarely seen, legendary snow leopard also lives.

Before leaving Karsha I went to see the local 'lord', the Karsha Lumpo. A tall, elegant, erudite man, father of five children and an old friend from my previous visits, he now recounted to me how as a child he had witnessed the discovery of an ancient grave. Maybe, he suggested, it was a Drok-pa grave.

It took us fifteen minutes to reach the site, a low ridge overlooking the sprawling central plain of Zanskar. Several rounded mounds were clearly visible, rising like nobs upon the ridge. The Karsha Lumpo led me to a shallow pit lined with rocks. 'It was here,' he explained, 'that they found bones and a few clay pots.' The hole was about six feet deep but not very wide. How I wished to have been able to excavate the other mounds.

The Karsha Lumpo then took me over to see the ruins of an old fortress which, he claimed, was associated with Zanskar's ancient past, 'Before the Tibetans came,' as he put it. There at the foot of a rocky spur were the pecked outlines of hundreds of little *chortens* beside numerous ibex carvings. Above this spot rose the remains of several thick walls. I could well imagine this once to have been an ancient Minaro camp.

From Karsha we carried on down the Zanskar River towards Pimo, where I had panned for gold in the very same sands that had over millenniums accumulated on the banks of the Indus to the north. Before reaching Pimo we left the trail to cross a suspension bridge formed of long strands of rope which stretched out 230 feet across the roaring Zanskar River which here is wider, deeper and faster flowing than the upper Indus in Ladakh. As we made our way across the suspension bridge Missy was horrified to appreciate that the ropes were made not of some strong fibre but of brittle plaited twigs of dwarf birch trees. This rope, that any child could have snapped in his hands, uncannily stood up to the tremendous longitudinal pull of the weight of those who crossed the bridge.

On the other side of the bridge lay Zangla, understandably a place rarely visited. Here lived the King of Zangla, an old man nearing 75, slim of build and with a toothless smile. On normal days he dressed in what most Europeans would have considered rags, keeping his fine red homespun gown for festive occasions. For five hundred years the King of Zangla's family had ruled their kingdom's four small impoverished villages. He was more of a father to the peasants than a regal figure and had, twenty years previously, returned to them the land that had once been his as king. He lived in a rambling adobe house whose chapel was adorned with fine gilt statues, the only true wealth of this remote, impoverished monarch. Yet what he lacked in splendour the king made up for in his knowledge of the land's customs and traditions, stretching back to the days when Tibetan soldiers coming east, preceding the nomads, had settled in this remote valley, intermarrying with or chasing away its earliest inhabitants, the fair-skinned ancestors of the present-day Minaro.

On a vertical crag above the village rises the ruins of the ancient castle of the kings of Zangla. It was here in 1823 that an amazing Hungarian, the first European to enter Zanskar, had studied for a year. This young man, by the name of Csomo de Koros, had one obsession all his life: he hoped to find, in Central Asia, the ancestors of his Hungarian people. Like myself he had looked to the East for clues to our ancient past. Penniless and lightly clad, taking the name of Sikander Beg (Mr Alexander), he left Hungary on foot in 1818. The next one hears of him is that he is travelling across Persia in disguise after having floated down the Tigris. In Tehran he borrowed money from some British officers before resuming his solitary journey, still calling himself Sikander Beg. In disguise he reached Bokhara, the heart of ancient Bactria, where he was stopped from going further east by Russian soldiers. Turning south, he ended up in Kabul. When Kabul became dangerous he entered, still in native dress, the Indian Punjab (before its conquest by the British). Koros now wanted to find a way to return to the Central Asian steppes, but the Himalayas lay in his path. Fearless of such an obstacle, he set out in 1820 for Kashmir and Ladakh. On his way, at Dras, he ran into the English explorer Moorcroft. We do not know exactly what went on between the two adventurous scholars, but it seems that Moorcroft told Csomo to shape up and learn Tibetan instead of chasing for his ancestors. He gave Csomo an early Latin–Tibetan dictionary, compiled by the Catholic priest Father Georgi and printed in Rome in 1762. He also gave Csomo a letter of recommendation to a learned monk who had married the widow of the King of Zangla. Thus began the scholarly career of Csomo de Koros, a man today acclaimed as the 'father of Tibetan studies', the first person to examine the vast body of Tibet's sacred literature.

It was strange to find myself at Zangla looking out upon the parched, tormented mountains of the western Himalayan highlands from the very window through which Koros had once peered. As he had pondered, I too now asked myself who were our ancestors. Had they really come from these mountains or had Koros and I both made a mistake? Sitting on the floor of his little cell I reflected that modern scholarship seems to have proven that Koros was mistaken in seeking the origin of the Hungarians in the Far East because linguistically, at least, Hungarian is neither a Turko-

Mongolian nor an Indo-European language but related to Finnish. One must assume therefore that Hungarians came from the north rather than the east. This being said, the plains of Hungary had seen the coming from the east of many invaders from central Asia.

Packing our bags on the back of a pony we bade goodbye to the old king and set off north to the monastery of Thonde at the foot of the rugged 18,150 foot Thonde-la pass.

The following day, having acquired another pony for Missy, we began the climb up the face of the Thonde-la out of the valley of Zanskar. As I panted ever upwards, exhausted yet elated by the altitude, I began to understand why since childhood I had been enthralled, first by the bison, than by Stone Age tools. My fascination with the amazing collective memory of the Himalayans which spanned thousands of years, with Herodotus' stories of the Eastern Amazons and the land of the gold-digging ants, I now saw to be part of the very essence of humanity. If 'a man without traditions was not man', as had been suggested to me one day in the jungles of Yucatan, perhaps we survived as a species largely because we had learnt to query the past, our survival dependent upon our ability to learn from past experience. Perhaps my curiosity was nothing more than an instinct, like the chase – an instinct for survival, the need to learn for oneself the knowledge acquired by past generations. The past is, after all, our only legacy. Maybe it was instinct that had driven me to the East to read its last messages.

I now knew it to be true that there did exist in the East fair children and long-nosed men, and I believed that the last heirs to our neolithic past were truly to be found here. Had it been worth while, I wondered, as I looked at Missy courageously hanging on to her saddle, and at Nordrop, like me perspiring heavily as we reached 18,000 feet. Slowly beneath us the world began to fall away, the distant peaks everywhere visible behind the horizon. We were reaching the pass, topped by a cairn that marked the link between men and the gods. Soon I heard Nordrop cry '*Ki-ki so-so*' as he reached the summit.

Looking back I could see the furrowed earth cleft in a thousand scars and ridges falling to valleys and plains where flowed silent rushing rivers, threads of gold across the moonscape. In vain I looked down from the pass for a sign that men lived here below, in vain I searched for a testimonial of what had been millenniums of occupation of this site by humans. All I could see, to the far horizon, was a silent succession of peaks, the immensity of nature at its most grandiose. Nature superb, neither kind nor cruel but totally indifferent to the creed and ideologies of those ambitious bipeds that had raised here a small cairn, there a stone; who, a little further on, had pecked a rock, in the hope perhaps that these little acts might provide lasting evidence of their spirit. Meagre efforts at conversation with infinity, the lone clues to our legacy.

Entering the edge of the great void of the Rupchu plateau, we passed the rotting carcass of a dead mule. Was it an omen? Buffeted by a freezing wind, yet burnt by the ultraviolet rays of the sun in the high, thin altitude, we stumbled down an eroded glacial valley, heading for the heart of the Rupchu highlands.

As we tramped on, I pondered again on the way of life of Stone Age man. My conviction that, contrary to popular belief, he lived in some abundance, must certainly have been true of the ancient Minaro in this land of ibex. Our own research, and that of certain prehistorians, allowed us to imagine that the men of each village preyed upon definite herds of ibex, which they might have treated somewhat as farmers today treat their domestic animals, following the ibex on their annual migration from the valley to the mountain tops and marking the limits of their territory with carved boulders. Looking up now I could see the patchwork of small green ibex pastures bordering the snow fields. During the summer the Minaro must have moved out in the open, sleeping, like my friends from Zanskar, not in tents, but under the stars.

On the high ridges of the mountains in the brief Himalayan summers are found not only medicinal plants and the poisonous aconite, but also a host of edible berries and vegetables. With Nordrop I had eaten wild peas collected at 15,000 feet. These peas, with furry pods, were no doubt the cousins of the domestic peas grown today in the area. The most common berries were a type of red currant found on the banks of the mountain streams that drain the melting snow off the summits. Whenever we came upon these bushes we gave them a close shave, stuffing the fruit into our mouths with a speed that reminded us that man is equipped with the perfect tools for plucking and picking. We are, after all, not only hunters but also gatherers by nature.

The streams would also have offered our forefathers an abundance of fish, among them Himalayan trout as well as the larger *massia*, the Himalayan salmon. In the highest regions the trout often congregate in clear pools, where they are easy to catch. Today they abound but are never eaten, because the Buddhists think it a hideous crime to take the life of one of the few living creatures that has no voice with which to cry out for help. The Minaro were probably not encumbered by such considerations.

They must also have relished mountain chickens, whose noisy cackles we often heard as we advanced. The size of a large pheasant, the colour of clay, they abound in the wilds of the less travelled sections of the western Himalayan highlands. They make such a noise that one is warned long in advance of their approach; they rarely fly, but hop along together, a whole brood of maybe fifteen birds at a time. These too have become taboo for the Buddhists.

Thus in summer neolithic man's stay upon the high slopes would have provided a rich and varied diet, from peas to roast mountain chicken and berries, not to mention roast ibex, which everyone who has tasted it declares to be the most savoury of all wild game.

As the winter cold began to set in the Minaro would have come slowly down to the relatively warmer sheltered valleys, collecting juniper wood to stockpile near the caves and huts in which they would spend the coldest months. With the first snows, they must have killed many hundred ibex whose carcasses they would hang up to dry and to freeze. These would keep all winter, so that when ice and snow made hunting too difficult, the Minaro would have then, as today, ample stores of dry or frozen meat.

That night sundown caught us in the wild gorge of a bounding torrent. We forded the freezing water and then set up camp, while Nordrop and our muleteer scoured the banks of the river for twigs and yak dung that became the base of a small fire around which we crowded. As we heated water to produce the salty tea that would dampen Nordrop's barley flour, we ate a few cold wheat cakes. Nordrop and the muleteer happily slept out in the open, sheltered only by the ponies' saddles, despite the cold at 16,000 feet.

The following morning we began descending the river bed that occasionally narrowed into a canyon dominated on all sides by fantastic castles, sculpted out of the cliffs by the wind. Red rocks contrasted with the pale blue water and the green of dwarf willows. Once, twice, three times, and eventually eighteen times, we had to take off our shoes and wade across the glacial stream, each crossing getting more and more dangerous as the river, swollen by its tributaries, got deeper and deeper. At first Missy could ride across the river, hanging on to the pony's mane, but soon this became impossible as the pony had to swim. I was preparing to cross the torrent once again when Nordrop grabbed my arm and in silence pointed to the mountain just above us. '*Skin*,' he said.

Automatically I searched for ibex carved rocks, but look as I did, I could see none on the near boulders.

'*Karé-ré?*' I asked, a little impatient. 'What is it?'

'*Di la,*' answered Nordrop, still pointing.

I followed his hand as it led up to the very summit of the mountain. Certainly too far to see anything.

'Ibex,' he repeated. 'A whole herd.'

I realized then he meant the live beast. Straining my eyes I saw in the far distance a small herd of ibex grazing. My heart beat as it rarely had. Was it from memories of the chase, or simply the fact that by now, as with the Minaro, ibex had begun to play in my life a role that far exceeded that of a mere animal? For me it had become a symbol, the ritual gift between gods and men.

As we carried on it seemed as if we were getting lost in the tormented bowels of the mountain. Peaks rarely appeared above the sheer walls of the river which enclosed us in shaded gullies. We were now in one of the more remote and unexplored regions of the Himalayas, in the very heart of the world's highest land mass. Here, at 15,000 feet, it seemed that man had no place, while animal life came as a surprise.

Towards evening, exhausted, we had to cross the river yet again, this time its icy flow reaching our stomachs. More travellers have died in Himalayan rivers than I liked to recall. Together Nordrop and I helped Missy across, her progress impaired by her steel braces without which she could no longer climb. It was folly, I thought, to have brought her here, in pursuit of what? A chance encounter with ibex, real ones and ibex of stone. I was lost in these uncomfortable thoughts, when suddenly we stumbled upon a bright red, painted *chorten*. Prayer flags dangled from branches on its summit, which was crested by a pair of ibex horns.

The sun was now slanting on the horizon, throwing golden light on to the barren mountains around us. Behind the shrine a dark fissure indicated a crack in the massive cliff. Was this a giant sacred cleft rock? I was surprised when Nordrop, dragging a pony, plunged down into the narrow crack as if entering a door into some underworld.

If there was ever a fairy passageway, this was it. After several miles in a dark gully, we slowly emerged into another world. The banks of the little stream that ran down the canyon began to widen, covered with thick grass, the first consistent vegetation we had seen for weeks. This grass soon turned into a marsh, lush with tall spiky clumps of sod. Gradually this broadened out until we were no more surrounded by crags and dry cliffs but by low rounded hills covered in green. Through the narrow secret door we had reached the edge of the great plains approaching the isolated village of Shadi. Already a few figures were coming out to greet us. Looks of amazement followed our strange little procession.

I in turn looked at the villagers, trying to read in their features traces of time and history. The men and women had sun-darkened faces, some nearly black, others dyed with goats' horn powder for protection against the deadly rays of the sun. Here too it seemed that nobody washed; yet the people were not Minaro for their features were undeniably Oriental. Before me were the western-most Tibetan nomads, Drok-pa hailing from the Far East, the vanguard of a slow invasion of the rightful home of the Minaro.

For the first time in years I felt a stranger among Tibetans. I now knew that deep down I was not a breeder of cattle but a Minaro made for the chasing of ibex. It was here in Shadi that we had lost the war for the control of Asia, a war that had begun in earnest less than a hundred years after Alexander the Great's conquest, in 246 BC, with the coming to power of Shi Hwang-ti. He, the first Universal Emperor of China, not only built the Great Wall but sent out into Mongolia 300,000 troops to attack and defeat the Hiung-nu, the ancestors of the Mongolian hordes. This battle and the building of the Great Wall marked the beginning of the greatest population movement in history, one that was to change the map of the world for ever. Once defeated, the Hiung-nu turned west and attacked the white and no doubt Aryan Yue-chi, who in turn fleeing west defeated the Saca or Scythians, who fled west into Afghanistan and India. Thus in domino fashion the early Aryans and other Caucasians of Asia were knocked westwards, starting in Europe what we know as the barbarian invasions that sent the Goths into Portugal and eventually the Mongols to the doors of Vienna.

Less often known is that this same movement sent the Tibetan nomads on their march west from the borders of China, sweeping the Minaro before them as they advanced across the great Tibetan plains infiltrating the entire Himalayas, sparing only the small Minaro community of Zanskar and those villages along the Indus. Shadi marked the ultimate front of this great migration towards the south-west.

Having visited the area and examined the people who had ousted the Minaro, the time had come for us to turn back, confident that at last our efforts would be crowned by the long-awaited permit to enter the villages along the Indus from which we had been barred for so long.

9

OPERATION IBEX

Back in Kargil we found two messages waiting for us. One was a reply from our request to Zail Singh, the other from our negotiations undertaken anew by Sheikh Abdullah. Both refused us the permits to travel to the Minaro villages.

Reading these messages again and again our hearts sank in bitter disappointment. If we had indeed made great progress in identifying the Minaro, there were still many unanswered questions. We had yet to locate the Greek El Dorado and identify the gold-digging ants. Certain as we were that the Minaro were truly the Dards mentioned by Herodotus we felt that the gold must at long last be within our reach.

I raged at being powerless to overcome a bureaucracy interested only in politics – the stupid politics of modern rivalries that had appropriated to the distant governments of Pakistan and India a portion of the globe that belongs to neither. Yet what could we do? Mrs Gandhi and Zail Singh, the Prime Minister and the President of India, had both turned down our appeals. There was no recourse. Perhaps there was after all, I thought, no more room for adventure in our modern world. So I believed as we reluctantly made our way back to Europe in late September 1981.

Missy was equally indignant that we were not to be allowed to pursue our harmless quest. 'Let's go anyway,' she suggested one day.

'Why not?' I heard myself reply. Thus was born our new plan.

I have always considered myself a law-abiding citizen, but now I asked myself what obliged me to abide by India's unjustified territorial claim over this area. It truly mattered little whether what we had now decided to undertake was legal or not. Come what may we would penetrate the Minaro's forbidden land. To do so we would go in disguise, were it only to see for an instant with our own eyes the lost horizon of their secret sanctuary.

Back in Europe this plan began to mature. Never again did we question the morality of our decision. There were, we knew, countless precedents for our chosen course of action. After all, Csomo de Koros, the Hungarian scholar, travelled in disguise, as also did the famed explorer Richard Burton. Was it not also disguised in the robes of a Tibetan woman that Alexandra David-Neel had reached Lhasa? The more we considered the matter, the better we were able to convince ourselves that what we now planned to undertake was justified.

Reaching a decision was much easier than carrying it out. We came to call our plan 'Operation Ibex'. From the very beginning we realized that in choosing this course of action we had landed ourselves in a somewhat lonely world. Fortunately, in my life of roaming the Himalayas I had always retained my independence. I was affiliated to no university, institution or government, and therefore had no one to whom I had to account for my actions. Concerning Missy, I had second thoughts. Should she come with me? 'Of course,' she exclaimed. 'It was my idea in the first place.'

Looking at us both in the mirror I decided that we made a very handsome couple, and a tall one at that, both being over six feet. I knew that I would be considered very tall for a Minaro man, but I was sure that my fluency in Tibetan would get me through, as it was most doubtful that any of the Border Security Force could speak any local languages. But what to do with Missy? Even if she dressed as a man her command of Tibetan certainly was not strong enough to get her through. And then there was the problem of her curly hair and spectacles; unbelievably myopic, Missy could hardly move without her glasses, not to mention her cumbersome knee braces. Reluctantly, Missy agreed that she could not come into restricted territory, although she knew how much I would need her in Ladakh to help bail me out of jail if I were caught or, preferably, to waylay any curious officials or police who might be following us.

We discussed our project for days and nights. One question

constantly arose in my mind; what if we get caught? To enter strategic border zones was a serious enough offence, but to cross one after having, on several occasions, been specifically refused permission by the highest authorities was a far worse crime. I certainly could not hope for any leniency from Mrs Gandhi. Then I thought about the army. There were supposed to be over a quarter of a million troops in Kashmir, of which perhaps half were there to control the strategic border area along the cease-fire line. I presumed that the army would deal severely with any breaches of their border regulations.

I imagined myself rotting in jail, dying of dysentery in a cold, dank cell; or sweltering somewhere in the Indian plains. I knew the Indians to be paranoiac about their restricted areas, of which today there are well over a dozen. Thus it is that one cannot travel to Nagaland, the Lacdive Islands or Assam without special permits; likewise the border areas of Tibet, the old North-west Frontier Agency, and portions of Sikkim and the Gharwal Himalayas are closed to all foreigners. And then there were the sensitive border zones of Ladakh: first Rupchu, then the Chang-tang up to the Chinese-held frontier; also Nubra which leads to the Karakoram Mountains; and last, but not least, the Minaro area north of the strategic road that leads from Srinagar to Leh.

We also had to bear in mind the traditional dislike of most Indian officials for foreigners, a legacy of colonialism; the natural delight of bossy bureaucrats in telling Europeans where they could or could not go. All this would weigh heavily against us in case of failure. I was not so naïve as to believe that in disguise I could carry out any sort of anthropological investigation. It was definitely out of the question to linger in villages full of Indian military personnel; I would immediately be singled out as a stranger, and a strange stranger indeed. Sometimes I would wake in the night and, thinking it all over, find it a foolish idea. What could I hope to accomplish by crossing the forbidden frontier?

But as I recalled the ants' gold, another voice would prod me on. Surely, if I were caught, Shiekh Abdullah would stand by me. After all, my failure to secure the permits was in a way his own. Certainly he must have been angered to see his strongest recommendations go unheeded by the Central Government, for he was the Chief

Minister of Kashmir, an autocrat, head of an Indian State with a strong independence movement. As the Sheikh had once whispered to Missy, 'You see, in regards to India, Kashmir is like a young woman, she wants to live alone, to be independent. But,' he added with a twinkle in his eye, 'this does not mean that she really dislikes her parents.'

To allay my fears and cheer myself up I re-read one of his messages addressed to the CID and DIC (the Indian political police):

'The Chief Minister, Sheikh Abdullah, has desired that the foreigners [Missy and I] may be recommended for grant of permit to undertake the research work, as their work is of purely academic nature and useful for the State.'

No, the Sheikh would not let me down.

But I also re-read, with a shudder, how Amnesty International had in 1979 lodged a complaint against torture and imprisonment in Kashmir, based on the 'allegations of the torture of some 48 army officers who had been arrested in the state of Jammu and Kashmir on charges of espionage'. Three of them had 'been tortured by being beaten on the soles of their feet', one of them had reportedly been subjected to 'burning with cigarettes and to having sharp objects inserted into his rectum'.

I remembered too the message 'SHOOT TO KILL', the miles of barbed wire, the rows and rows of Nissen huts, the guards, the patrols and the Border Security Force.

To counteract all this was the excitement. After all, I had yearned for adventure since I was a child. Perhaps this was my chance to test my courage for a just cause.

In Paris we began working on my disguise. It was impossible, all agreed, for Missy to pass herself off as a Minaro, either man or woman. As for myself, being taller than any Minaro, I would have to learn to reduce my size.

'What gives most people away is their walk,' commented a friend of mine, an actress, who agreed to give me 'walking' lessons. Passers-by in Paris stared at me as I slunk along the streets, hunched over and, on my friend's advice, trying to 'walk as if every step is your last'.

The plan was that I should disguise myself to look like a Minaro, to fool not other Minaro but the Indian police, military security officers and border patrols. For the most part these were people from central India who no doubt considered the Minaro an odd lot. Being yet another Aryan with European features I hoped to have little cause to worry. For once my big nose and grey eyes were no problem. My skin was very pale, however, much lighter than most sun-tanned Minaro, so I would have to dye my face. Likewise I would need to dye my hair to hide the grey streaks at my temples, an unusual feature among the Minaro.

It was already summer in Paris when we began to finalize our plans. First we would go to Pakistan where I could have 'native' clothes made without arousing any suspicion. This would also give us an opportunity to study the Shina-Minaro on the Pakistani side of the cease-fire line. We would then walk over the frontier at Amritsar into India, thereby avoiding Delhi and any possible encounters with the central authorities. Once in India we would proceed to Kargil where I would try to talk some guides into taking me across the 'inner line' into Minaro territory. This last, and most crucial part of the plan, the finding of guides, had to be left open.

Meanwhile I began to investigate techniques for dyeing my skin and hair. As the latter was thinning I also contemplated the purchase of a wig, and maybe a moustache. In Paris most of the shops are closed in August, particularly the *drogueries* where I had hoped to buy walnut juice (usually used for dyeing furniture) to darken my skin. This would normally have been easy to find, but with all the small paint shops closed I had to search the large department stores for walnut dye. I could not find the real thing, however; all wood dyes contained the warning 'this is a chemical product'. I now had visions of myself dyed for life, or of my skin peeling off under the effects of some horrible poisonous ingredient. Hunt as we did we never found any simple, old-fashioned walnut dye.

At the same time I scoured the big stores for wigs and moustaches. In desperation I tried on pigtails, pony-tails and hairpieces under the knowing smiles of salesgirls. 'Is it for a fancy dress party?' they asked. I had trouble explaining that I wanted to look like a Minaro. Nothing seemed to fit. 'You had better wear a hat,' said Missy, as I tried on another ludicrous nylon hairpiece.

I then gingerly entered beauty parlours. 'How can I quickly tan my skin?' I asked sheepishly. I found two alternatives: one was 'Man Tan', a lotion which it was claimed would darken me 'as desired' with repeated applications; the other was to use theatre make-up, grease paint, but this obviously would not last.

As for moustaches, all I could find were huge, woolly affairs fit only for birthday parties.

Deeply frustrated, I was finally directed to the 'Impasse de l'Industrie', a small arcade in the 10th arrondissement, a neighbourhood full of wholesale shops for hairdressers and barbers. Here, by the dozens, were barbers' swivel chairs, combs, wigs, scissors, driers, curlers and shampoos. Finally I found a moustache that struck my fancy and made me look like my friend Dorje Namgyal. In the meantime Missy bought cans of spray-on hair dye and a pot of moustache glue, and a friend of mine made an appointment with his somewhat fancy hairdresser for the dyeing of my eyebrows, a delicate operation.

As I went about making these purchases it all seemed rather a farce, yet I constantly had a dry feeling in my throat. I knew that it would no longer be a joke out there on the cease-fire line. I had to admit that I would never make a good spy, for I already felt guilty as I slouched about Paris in my best Minaro gait.

Then there was the question of whether I should take a camera. Immediately I thought of those little spy cameras, just the right size to conceal in a prayer wheel – an old trick of the British secret 'native agents'. These were trained Nepalese and Bhutanese who, around 1870, were sent out by the British to map the remote, forbidden valleys of Tibet, Nepal and Bhutan. The notes they took were concealed in prayer wheels, while thermometers (which were thrust into boiling water to record altitudes) were hidden in their walking sticks. It was these agents who, known only by their initials, made the first accurate maps of the more remote parts of the Himalayas, maps which are still used today. Known as the Indian Survey ¼ inch, they are now 'Classified' by the Indian government although one can buy copies of them in England. However, I was unable to secure detailed maps of the region I wished to penetrate and had to make do with a larger scale 'Classified' American copy.

I now found myself confronted with all the problems of a professional spy: how to smuggle into India my moustache, make-up, small camera and map. All this did much to increase my guilt and fears. I had constant visions of myself behind bars, and at times even saw myself before a firing squad.

By the end of August we were ready to leave for Pakistan with our tents, sleeping bags and usual equipment dissimulating my less conventional gear.

On arrival in Islamabad, Pakistan's new capital, we were confronted with a new set of problems as I sought permission to penetrate the Pakistani side of the cease-fire line. A further complication was that I lost my two front teeth on arrival, giving me, a little too soon, the enchanting smile of a suspicious-looking Minaro. Hasty repairwork in the makeshift cabinet of a missionary clinic restored my appearance as Missy and I began investigating the historical sites that recalled Alexander's visit to Pakistan.

Forty miles from Rawalpindi and Islamabad rise the ruins of Taxila, the ancient capital of northern Pakistan, visited by Alexander. Much has been written about Alexander's campaign in India, yet there are still many unanswered questions as to whom exactly he had encountered there. Could he have met the early Minaro? Little or no anthropological details about the people he met filter through the texts of his various historians: Arrian, Diodorus, Curtius or Plutarch. Once Alexander's troops had got as far as the Kabul River, in present day Afghanistan, they had reached the watershed of the upper Indus. They would doubtless have expected, as does any modern traveller or explorer, that on entering India they would be met by a strange, dark-skinned people, signalling a different world. One can therefore understand the surprise of the Macedonian troops, and Alexander himself, when, on the banks of the Swat River, a tributary of the Indus, they came upon the fair-skinned inhabitants of the town of Nysa. Today Nysa has been identified as standing at the foot of the three-peaked Koohinoor hills in the valley of Swat. Reports about this town vary from one historian to the next, but what is clear is that the inhabitants of Nysa had very fair skin and pale eyes. All agreed that they were more like Greeks than Persians or Indians. Who were they?

The historian Arrian claims that they were possibly Greek

soldiers who had come with the Thebian god Dionysus who, as all knew, claimed to have travelled to India. The noted expert on Alexander, W. W. Tarn, suggested that they were 'descendants of Darius's Greek mercenaries'. Alexander himself was happy to proclaim the inhabitants of Nysa to be descendants of Dionysus' Greek soldiers in order to show that he was about to go further east than had the god himself. As a result Alexander let the Nysians go free, remain independent, and retain their autocratic form of government. It is amusing to note that Alexander's readiness to declare the fair inhabitants of India to be descendants of Greek troops was duplicated two thousand years later by the British, who on first entering the foothills of Swat and the nearby Chitral valley found a fair-skinned people, the Kailash, or Kafirs of the Hindu Kush. These, like the Minaro, they erroneously declared to be the descendants of Alexander's Greek troops, for lack of a better explanation.

It is my deepest conviction that neither the present-day, fair-skinned, European-looking Kailash nor the Nysians seen by Alexander in Swat were Greek. They were, I believe, some of the earliest inhabitants of Asia, an aboriginal people akin to the Minaro who had found refuge in remote valleys.

Travelling up the Swat valley, Alexander encountered yet more fair people, variously called the Assacenians, Aspasians or Gureans. He fought them first in a memorable battle at Massaga, a fortress which has never been located. Then, leaving the Swat valley, the Greek conqueror moved over to the valley of the Indus, slightly north-west of Taxila. To Alexander, still recovering from a wound he had received at Massaga, it appeared essential to defeat the so-called Assacenians, Aspasians and Gureans. Having stormed one of their strongholds called the 'rock of Aornus' Alexander pursued them further up the Indus, encountering considerable resistance along the way. Deliberating as to who these people could have been, it occurred to me that they were one and the same. *Asva* means horse in Sanskrit, and *gurre* is horse in Kashmiri; it may be no coincidence that *asp* or *apsh* in Shina and Minaro still today means horse.

I hoped to find out whether there was indeed any connection between the Minaro and the original Aspasians encountered by Alexander as I proceeded north to visit the regions adjoining the upper Indus where Shina is still spoken by nearly 100,000 people. It was vital for me to establish to what extent the Shins of Pakistan, now all Muslims, were related to the Minaro of Ladakh and Zanskar.

In a small plane I flew with Missy up the Indus, heading for Skardo. The wings of our aircraft almost touched the peaks that crowded the great river. It was no place in which to venture with an army; Alexander had been right to turn back. Two thousand odd years later it was here in these very gorges that the British had met their most stubborn resistance in India, fighting until 1939 and even later the fierce Shina-Minaro of Chilas whom they never fully subdued. Still today, we had been warned, certain of these hill tribes are armed and do not hesitate to shoot at foreigners foolish enough to enter their villages uninvited.

Flying over these villages we followed the Indus north until it suddenly turned east around 26,600 foot Nanga Parbat into Baltistan, the Tibetan-speaking province of Pakistan along the upper Indus. Baltistan's capital, Skardo, lies in a lunar landscape set between the Karakoram range and the Himalayas. On our way from the airport we bounced over sand dunes as we drove to the bazaar set among willow trees at the foot of the Tibetan-style residence of the Rajas of Skardo. We were now in that part of Kashmir that had been overrun in 1947 by Pakistani troops. The local people, although Muslim, still speak pure, archaic Tibetan, as they do in Kargil which lies only 80 miles upstream.

In Skardo I sought permission to travel up the Indus to the cease-fire line, curious to see if there were any Minaro settlements along the way. In spite of the strong letters of recommendation I had, the permit was refused, and we had to content ourselves with interviewing local people. These interviews confirmed that there were three Minaro villages on the southern bank of the Indus, but that they were populated by believers in Allah, unlike the Buddhist Minaro on the other side of the line. What was interesting was that the people of Skardo differentiated these Minaro villages from the other villages south of the Indus, inhabited by Shina-speaking people who in language, if not in customs, are related to the Minaro.

While I was in Skardo I found a tailor to make me a pair of oversized, baggy grey trousers, such as those worn by people in Kargil. I also managed to buy a vast shirt whose tails fell well down over my knees.

With my wardrobe complete we went off to visit the nearby valley of Shigar, which runs up to the Karakoram. There the Baltis (inhabitants of Baltistan), who speak Tibetan, had much fairer skin than their Mongolian-featured cousins from Ladakh. It seemed that the earliest inhabitants had merely adopted the Tibetan language without, apparently, intermarrying with them. The Baltis, I could only deduce, were probably directly related to the Minaro. This seemed to be confirmed by the numerous stones we encountered carved with ibex, similar to those we had found all over Ladakh, and also by Minaro oral tradition that says they once settled in Shigar. This visit hardened my conviction that in the Minaro I had found the oldest survivors of what must have been a large Asiatic group of Caucasian people of neolithic traditions.

Before leaving Skardo we were fortunate in securing permission to cross the Deosai Plain, an area generally forbidden to foreigners. In a government jeep we pulled out of the Indus valley through a narrow gorge where we saw several altars covered with ibex horns. Very soon the trail began to climb until we reached 13,000 feet, the last bend taking us up to a breathtaking view. Before us stretched a vast prairie-like expanse of almost flat, rolling plains. This was the Deosai, a totally uninhabited plateau some fifty miles in diameter covered with small shrubs and wild flowers, criss-crossed by rivulets and marshy patches. All around, beyond the horizon, rose barren snow peaks. It was as if some giant had grown tired of the Himalayan sea of jagged ranges and had made a vast clearing, an island of level land fit only for the gods.

As we rolled over the plain we soon found that in fact the gods shared this abode with a few select animals who could withstand the ferocious nine-month winter. Here were Himalayan bears, and marmots, marmots in their hundreds. To traverse this wild expanse, we were travelling with another jeep which carried several Shina-speaking officials. They were armed with rifles, out mercilessly to shoot anything that moved. Hearing our approach the marmots came out of their burrows and stood perched up on their hind legs, signalling the alarm with short, high-pitched whistles.

I asked our Shina companions if they knew of any legends concerning marmots, and was told the following story. One day a man lost his horse on this plain, just at the beginning of winter. Desperate, he feared that his horse would die of hunger or freeze to death in the snow. To his surprise, next spring he found the horse alive and well; it had been fed by a marmot from the store of grass which the little animals keep underground. Instead of being grateful, however, the owner destroyed the marmots' burrows. This explains why marmots stand up and whistle in anger whenever they see a man, which they never do when approached by a horse or other animal.

I inquired if there was any gold on the Deosai and was told that some was to be found in the beds of two little streams that ran down into the Astor valley. Gold! Anxiously I asked everyone I met in the Astor valley if they knew any stories about gold-digging ants . . . but no one knew anything. Some people in the upper Astor valley told me that the otters in the river were believed to have gold in their stomachs, although no one had ever found any.

Returning down the Astor valley to the Indus, we continued our search for ibex stones. We found many of these, but none of the Shina-speaking people knew who had carved them or what they represented. Later we found more rocks carved with ibex along the Indus, and around Gilgit and Hunza, but no one there claimed to know anything about them either.

We continued searching, trying to determine just how far west the carved rocks and stone altars could be found, the last vestiges of the religion still practised by the Minaro, yet forgotten by their Shina cousins of Gilgit and Astor as a result of their brutal con-version to the Muslim faith. In Gilgit I was anxious to see the ways in which the Shins there still resembled the Minaro, since the Minaro of the Indus claimed that they had originally come from Gilgit in a herding migration under the leadership of Gil Sangye, the Lion of Gilgit.

Anthropological studies in this region by Professor Karl Jettmar and others have revealed that the Shins, before their conversion to Islam, had professed a faith somewhat similar to that of the Minaro, a religion in which the ibex, the use of juniper, and standing stones played an important part. The Shins of northern Pakistan, it was clear, were once part of the same people, but they had lost their customs and ethnic purity through numerous foreign invasions of their territory. One of the first of these had been the Greeks under Alexander, followed later by the Saca, the Ghandarians, the Tibetans and, more recently, the Muslim Pathans from the south. The only people in this part of the world to have preserved their traditions and escaped conversion to Islam were the Kafirs, 'infidels' of the upper Chitral valley, known as the Kailash, whose pale complexions and European appearance strikingly resemble the Minaro. However the Kailash, over the years, developed a far more complex religion than that of the Minaro, although similar to it in some respects, particularly concerning being pure or ritually clean.

Just north of Gilgit stands the small but famous kingdom of Hunza, a popular Shangri-la whose inhabitants are renowned for their longevity. Hunza's capital Baltit has been renamed Karimabad, after the Aga Khan, for its people are Ismaili Muslims, beneficiaries of the generosity of their famous leader. The people of Hunza speak Burushashki, a language quite unrelated to Indo-European languages such as Shina. For this reason some scholars have proclaimed them to be the aboriginal population of the area, in other words to have resided there before the Shins and, pre-sumably, the Minaro. I do not believe this to be the case for several reasons, one being that the local Hunza holy men, when in a trance, actually speak Shina. This and other facts, such as the absence of Burushashki words in village names in the upper Indus, seem to indicate that they were but one of the several peoples to have moved into the region in relatively recent times, the Hunza people no doubt hailing from across the Karakoram, having come by the major trade route along which their villages still stand.

However fascinating was our visit to Pakistan it was constantly overshadowed by the anxiousness surrounding our project. It was time for us to go to India and attempt to carry out our secret mission.

10

THE DEATH
OF THE LION

Our hearts beating nervously, Missy and I walked into India across the Lahore-Amritsar frontier, the only road connection between India and Pakistan. To enter India this way the traveller has to go through a comic opera routine, the border posts on either side of the frontier being separated by a distance of over one mile. In order to cross this no man's land one first has to hire Pakistani porters to carry one's bags on top of their heads for the first half-mile. At the actual frontier, delineated by a wide white line, they drop the bags and push them over the line with their feet; on the other side of the line one hires Indian porters to complete the second half-mile. In this way the frontier officials do not have to look each other in the eye.

Terribly anxious and filled with guilt, I was sure the customs officials would find my false moustache, funny clothes, hair dye and maps. Ignoring these, they seemed interested only in our expensive photographic equipment, fortunately taking no notice of my cheap little spy camera. Clear at last, we headed in a taxi for Amritsar, famed city of the Golden Temple, the spiritual home of the turbanned Sikhs. From there we took a plane to Srinagar.

The day after our arrival I made a simple but important discovery, that the Kashmiris living around Lake Wahur just north of Srinagar called the hill people to the north of them by the name of Darade or Darada! Amazingly enough it seems this simple fact was never noted by all those generations of scholars who had painstakingly searched for the origin of the name used by Herodotus. To my astonishment I now found that the northern Kashmiris still today use the name Darade when referring to the hill people 'who wear wool', the herders who live in the valleys and grazing lands leading to the Deosai – people whose main town is Gourais or Gurres, meaning horse, possibly the home of the Gureans or Aspasians whom Alexander had fought on the Indus. In other words the Gureans were also known as Darade. And these Darade or Gureans are Shina-speaking, related to the Minaro! This was an exciting, unexpected discovery, one more indication that the Minaro were no doubt the Dards of Herodotus.

Herodotus, and others after him, had simply used the northern Kashmiri term to describe the wild, horse-riding people of the upper Indus, a land abounding in gold. If I had so far failed to find the gold-digging ants at long last I knew that I was definitely on the right track.

A few days after our arrival we were deeply saddened to learn that Sheikh Abdullah was very ill, having suffered another heart attack.

In low spirits we combed the bazaar for final provisions. Among the items on our list was a toothbrush for dyeing my sideburns, and green walnuts from which to make a paste for staining my skin. At every turn we ran into people and officials we knew, all asking where we were planning to go. 'Back to Zanskar,' I replied guiltily. I have never been a good liar and now found myself caught in the web of my own conspiracy.

My final plans were still a little confused. How could I penetrate the forbidden zone, what route should I take? I contemplated buying a yak and, posing as a herder, leading it all the way to the first Minaro village; in this guise, speaking Tibetan, I thought I might fool the border officials. (This idea, I must confess, was not original, being based on a film I had once seen about a Frenchman who had escaped, unquestioned, through Germany leading a cow.) I felt the idea was a good one, especially as yaks are rather awe-inspiring; if I stuck to my yak I hoped that no one would call me in for questioning. But how to find the way? I would need a companion. I wondered if I could take my old friend Nordrop, for as a resident of Ladakh he would be allowed into parts of the cease-fire zone, but I realised that if we were caught Nordrop would also be likely to suffer imprisonment, or worse. I decided that I should in no way implicate Nordrop in my plan. I had to find someone else, but who? I still had no answer when we left the Srinagar valley on the first available bus to Kargil.

As we travelled along the all too familiar strategic highway over the Zoji-la pass, all now seemed different, filled as we were by a feeling of guilt and illegitimacy. Every soldier, every military vehicle we encountered on the way aggravated these feelings.

More than ever before I saw Ladakh as a military stronghold. The route into Kargil was cut at several points by checkpoints where Missy and I were forced to register our names and show our passports. Here and there were enormous billboards reminding foreigners not to stray from the main road, declaring that violators would be arrested and prosecuted. The badges of the Border Security Force on the soldiers' uniforms made me feel that they had been especially assigned to follow me. For the first time, I became fully aware of the immense military force in Ladakh: soldiers from Rajput regiments, the Jammu Brigade, the Ladakhi Scouts, the Dogra Company, the Gharwhal Rifles, Ghurkas with their deadly *khukris* and burly Sikhs in their turbans. A whole army there for one sole purpose, to protect their northern border zone, the very area that I intended to infiltrate. The situation in Afghanistan which had led America to arm Pakistan had that year made India reinforce her border. Suddenly I became very interested in the soldiers' weapons, their guns and sub-machine guns, as if they were all aimed at me. Decidedly, I did not have the nerves of a spy.

I was still very much on edge when we finally passed the last checkpost at Dras and lumbered into Kargil behind a military convoy. How I now hated the place! Kargil, where I had spent so many days desperately waiting for that permit. Kargil with its dirty bazaar and huge military camp blocking the horizon to the north, cutting me off from where the Minaro villages lay.

Unfortunately I had acquired over the years a certain notoriety in Kargil. The shopkeepers, police and the District Commissioner all knew me. No sooner had I disembarked with Missy than we were surrounded by friends – or would they all too soon become enemies, I wondered? At all costs I had to behave normally as we headed for the dak bungalow and our old friend, Mr Kakpori. To my immense relief he was away in Srinagar.

That night, before the town's generator was turned off, Missy and I examined our maps behind closed curtains. How many times had I already pored over them, trying to visualize what the terrain would be like. The geography was simple enough. The Indus River ran east to west and met the strategic Srinagar–Leh highway at the Khalatse bridge, the river and the road forming a triangle whose third side was the Suru River. Just before entering the Indus the Suru River crosses the cease-fire line. Within that forbidden triangle, along both sides of the Indus, were the Minaro villages. Somehow I would have to enter this triangle, around which were no less than four large military garrisons, while within there were, I understood, over a dozen smaller military posts. Perhaps up to fifty or seventy thousand troops were stationed in this small, highly strategic area.

Entering the triangle was a small military road used to supply the army outposts. This road, on the outskirts of Kargil, crossed the vast, barbed-wire enclosed compound of the local military head-quarters. It then traversed, by the Hambuting-la pass, the mountain range that separated Kargil from the Indus before reaching the town of Batalik, a military outpost on the banks of the Indus. Batalik is a Muslim Minaro community, just a few miles downstream from the village of Dartzig, the first of the Buddhist Minaro villages. Near Dartzig, a bridge crossed the Indus and the road led to Garkund, the home of my Minaro friend Dorje Namgyal. I imagined that this bridge would be at least as heavily guarded as the Khalatse bridge further upstream. How would I stand a chance crossing the bridge to reach Garkund, even leading a yak!

I knew that several times a week there was a bus along this military road serving some of the Minaro villages. (It was this very link that menaced the Minaro's customs and traditions; before dynamite enabled the building of this road it had been practically impossible to follow the gorges of the Indus into their territory.) Could I manage to smuggle myself aboard this bus in disguise? For some time I had contemplated this alternative, with a plan to bandage my face and fake a toothache. But I knew that, like the other passengers, I would have to get off the bus at each checkpost. I would be questioned, and the authorities, as well as my fellow passengers, would find me highly suspect. I then thought that perhaps I could talk a Minaro into passing me off as his half-wit brother (I had even practised making the appropriate grunts), but this was hardly likely to fool a busload of his own villagers. I had to think of something better.

Looking at the rugged mountains that separated me from the

Indus I also abandoned the idea of dragging along a yak. In Kargil, for the first time, I fathomed the folly of what I was about to do. This was not a simple case of sneaking across a border but of attempting to enter a heavily garrisoned military zone, and this in a terrain whose topography alone made it a natural trap, obliging one to cross nature's own checkposts: high passes or narrow gullies, outside of which there were no other passages. I would surely get caught, and then there would be no alternative but prison. For the first time I contemplated abandoning the whole project.

To cheer myself up I remembered the open letter I had left behind, addressed to a friend in Paris. In it I had explained that my mission was purely cultural, elaborating upon how I had been driven to my decision and how strongly I felt that political and military considerations should not be allowed to obstruct benign anthropological investigation. Were I caught, this letter was to be published in the press, while I hoped my friend would also ask the French authorities to intervene on my behalf, on the basis of something like the universal freedom of cultural information. It all sounded rather pompous and silly, but was of some comfort as I weighed my options there in Kargil. Missy, in the meantime, had found out that if I were indeed jailed it was she who would have to bring me my daily meals, as was the custom. Together we laughed at that, but our laughter did not ring true. We were still relying on the intervention of Sheikh Abdullah, a hope that was to be shattered all too soon in a very tragic way.

Two days later, when the generator had just been turned off and we were about to go to sleep, there came a banging at our door and the familiar ring of Mr Kakpori's voice. He had just returned by jeep from Srinagar with his beautiful Ladakhi wife and infant son. Kakpori seemed in a state of great agitation, for he already knew what we would learn only the next morning: that Sheikh Abdullah, the Lion of Kashmir, was dead.

'And where are you planning to go this year?' he asked, unaware of just how embarrassing this question was.

After a long explanation about how we were here to join Nordrop I told him that we planned to go up the Suru valley to record and photograph the inscription we had found the previous year, near the giant statue of Chamba (Buddha) just outside the village of

Kartsé. Missy and I had previously agreed that this was to be our 'cover' plan.

'Then we intend to return to Zanskar,' I continued unconvincingly.

The following morning, standing on the porch of the bungalow, I looked out across the Suru valley. Opposite me the brown, parched banks of the river rose to an equally barren plateau; this was the military camp fenced in with barbed wire. A helicopter was taking off from just below the hill in an enormous cloud of dust. As the dust settled I noticed that something was different. Finally I realized that 'SHOOT TO KILL' was gone! Was this a good omen? Or was it simply that some military commander had been convinced that such a slogan was not exactly good publicity for tourism? Behind the hill reared the jagged crests of a massive range, the range that I would soon have to cross to reach the Indus.

As the helicopter flew away I walked down to the bazaar. A crowd had gathered at the crossroads, and I noticed tattered black flags hanging from the roof tops and telephone poles. Then I heard the news. 'Sheikh Abdullah has died, the Sheikh is dead!' My heart sank. I was deeply saddened by the death of this great man, to whom I owed so much for his continued encouragement of my work over the years. From him I had received far more understanding and kindness than from any other official in India. Rather than seeing his death as a possible setback to our plans, I felt that in proceeding I would in a way be acting according to his wishes. For he alone had understood the importance of our study and appreciated how time was of the essence for the completion of our research on the Minaro, holders of the key to the ancient history and beliefs of his own beloved state.

The loudspeaker in the bazaar declared a period of three days' official mourning. Many people were worried as to what would happen in the wake of the great leader's death. I heard that the Indian army had been discreetly placed on alert. Probably sensing his imminent death, and in the desire to ensure a peaceful transition, the Sheikh had only a few weeks before named his son Farouq as his successor. Now everyone wondered if Farouq would have the same ability as his father in keeping peace in the turbulent Vale of Kashmir.

My plan now was to try to find Minaro villagers in Kargil whom I could hire as porters and guides to travel up the Suru river with us to where we would record the ancient inscription we had found the year before. In the course of this mission I hoped I would be able somehow to secure their confidence and collaboration, and that perhaps they would agree to lead me into their forbidden homeland. On our map I had begun to draw a vague itinerary. Leaving the statue and its inscription we would take a difficult, circuitous trail that leads over the 15,750 foot Rusi-la pass and then over the somewhat lower Sapi-la pass back around to the strategic road. At this point I would leave Missy somewhere in a side valley with Nordrop. I would then set off in disguise along the military road to where it crossed the village of Lotsum. From there I hoped to be able to travel, still in disguise, up a narrow valley towards the high pass that led over to the Indus and the heart of Minaro territory. This plan, of course, depended upon finding a guide or guides willing to risk the journey, and my being able to evade detection within the heavily guarded strategic triangle.

Hoping that Nordrop would stay and look after Missy, I sent a message for him to join us as usual in Kargil.

As I walked through the Kargil bazaar, past the tiny stalls selling pots and pans, bolts of cloth and grapes from Minaro villages, I reflected that it was getting late in the season – it was now the eighth of September, harvest time, which perhaps was why I could not find any Minaro in the bazaar. In desperation I went to the office of the local transport company housed in a dismal, half-abandoned building where I had once found a Minaro family squatting on the second floor. This time I only found two Ladakhis who had settled into a dirty room and were brewing salty tea. I sat down on the floor for a chat. They were pleasantly surprised that I could speak their language, and as usual I was delighted to talk to local people about their villages and listen to their tales.

This encounter was to prove fruitful. When I went back to see the Ladakhis next day, after having spent the entire morning hanging around the bazaar waiting for Nordrop, I noticed, to my intense delight, that three Minaro were sitting in an adjacent room. I walked in on them rather clumsily, and began chatting in Tibetan. They told me that they were from the village of Dartzig and that they were in Kargil to sell dried apricots. After we had savoured a few apricots, they went out and I rushed back to the dak bungalow to tell Missy.

'Do you think I can ask them to come with us?'

'Wait a little longer,' she suggested. 'Nordrop will turn up soon.'

Looking at my map I appreciated that Dartzig, being on the southern side of the Indus, was probably the easiest Minaro village to reach. This was good news, as I had become convinced that it would be nearly impossible to cross the strategic bridge and go to the Minaro villages on the other side.

When the next morning Nordrop had still not turned up, I decided to go back to the transport building with Missy. I could not find the Minaro, and the door to the room where they had been was now padlocked. Very anxious that I had missed my only chance of finding Minaro in Kargil I sat down with my Ladakhi friends and had some more salty tea. To my great relief the Minaro soon turned up. They stuck their heads round the door, so we bade them come in and we all sat in a huddle around a smoky Primus stove, sucking dried apricots and drinking tea.

We must have appeared an unusual group: the Ladakhis in their red gowns, and Missy impeccably smart, looking as if she had just walked out of a fashionable sports shop, in contrast to our Minaro friends who were dressed in rags. Yet they were most startling because they looked so much like us with their long noses and European features. One of them, whom I later learned was named Sonam, greatly resembled a Scots friend of mine, sheepish grin and all. Sonam's nose and chin were very long and thin, and his deep-set eyes twinkled; I expected him to speak English with a Scottish accent at any moment, but he chatted away in Ladakhi, speaking the language fluently like most Minaro. Sonam's light brown wavy hair came almost to his shoulders, giving him a rakish, rather hippy appearance. The second Minaro, named Tashi, seemed older, maybe 40; he wore a red, blue and green knitted cap which, I later learnt, hid the fact that he was partially bald, a very rare state in this part of the world. Just as some people in the West try to hide their baldness by combing their side hair across the top of their heads, he had his side hair divided into two sections and braided, the braids forming a strange sort of headband across the top of his head. His features, the eagle-like nose in particular, gave him the distinguished appearance of a European aristocrat, although his roughly shaven beard, strange coiffure and filthy clothes erased any further semblance of elegance. The third member of the party looked just like Sonam and was, I later learned, his brother.

Having downed the ritual three cups of salty tea, which frequently tastes like bad bouillon, we all rose. Leaving the Ladakhis I went with the Minaro to their room and asked them if they would consider being my porters on an expedition up the Suru valley. Taken aback, and a little suspicious, all three eyed me for a while and then spoke among themselves in Minaro.

'How much will you pay?' they finally asked.

'Twenty-five rupees a day,' I answered, this seeming a fair price.

'*Yapo*, good,' they answered in Ladakhi. 'Two of us will come, but first we will have to finish selling our apricots and that will take at least two more days.' I explained to them that this was fine, since I was waiting for a friend of mine, a lama from Zanskar, who would come with us.

It all seemed a little too good to be true when I realized that I had two Minaro ready to accompany me. All we needed now was for Nordrop to arrive. But the following day, and the next, there was still no sign of him. Desperate, I sent out yet more messages to Zanskar, with truck drivers, tourists and monks. Two days after our meeting with the Minaro I went back to the bus terminal to make final arrangements. They were nowhere to be found. To all appearances they had forgotten us or, perhaps, had better things to do. So now we were without guides and without Nordrop.

In the interim, quite by accident, I ran into the District Commissioner and the local head of police at the dak bungalow. Drinking tea with them I could not but wonder how they would react if I were brought back in handcuffs a week or so later, accused of spying.

To help calm my nerves while waiting for the Minaro and Nordrop to turn up, I killed time in the bazaar by discreetly buying other garments to supplement my disguise; a second-hand pair of brown army gym shoes and a cheap, oversized sweater. I also acquired a wretched-looking balaclava cap that seemed a fitting rival to the ones I had seen on the heads of our elusive friends from Dartzig. In the bazaar I remembered the advice of my actress friend and began closely observing how the local people walked, taking note of how they slouched, dragging their feet which were pointed out duck fashion, and the way they dangled their arms, imitating their movements when I was sure no one was watching.

There was still no sign of Nordrop and I was growing increasingly nervous when I ran into our Minaro friends. 'Where have you been?' I asked anxiously. They acted a bit stupid, then explained that they could not come with me as they still had business to do. They were accompanied now by two beautiful Minaro girls with long, pale faces and big hazel eyes. It appeared that my friends had still more sacks of apricots to sell and were anxious to busy themselves in the bazaar. Hastily I explained that it did not matter if we waited a few more days as my friend had still not shown up. They seemed pleased with the extension and set off about their business.

Strolling through the bazaar for the umpteenth time I caught sight of rugged-looking European trekkers with their backpacks and dusty clothes. They looked at me with what I took to be a sneer, probably because I looked like just another tourist on a package tour. How I longed to tell them my plans and share my anxieties with them, but refrained from doing so. I was on my way back to the dak bungalow when a tall man wearing clean, well pressed brown trousers and a flashy sports shirt grabbed my arm. What did he want, I wondered, taking him to be an Italian doctor on holiday.

'What is this?' he said abruptly, in impeccable English. 'You want to hire my friends?'

'What?' I stuttered, completely taken back. I then noticed a little behind him the smiling, Scottish face of Sonam, and the rather more austere look of Tashi, our men from Dartzig.

'Come, let's have some tea,' said the man in a rather bossy voice, leading me into the Blue Hotel, a dingy shack on the main street of the bazaar, its tearoom protected from the dust of the interminable military convoys by a few old rags flapping in the breeze. When we had seated ourselves the 'Italian doctor' looked me in the eyes and said, 'Now where is it you want to go?' adding in an aggressive tone, 'and how much are you going to pay these men?'

Still taken back, I answered, 'Twenty-five rupees a day.'

'Not enough,' said the stranger. 'You pay sixty rupees, all right?' The man then turned and to my surprise spoke to Sonam in fluent Minaro!

Having little time to collect my thoughts I countered with, 'Fifty rupees, and that's a lot.'

Swiftly the man jumped to his feet, patted Sonam and Tashi on the back and having said, 'All right,' disappeared as quickly as he had come, leaving me alone with my guides.

'Well,' I said, 'fifty rupees a day, but the pay starts the day after tomorrow when Nordrop is here.' I then gave each man an advance in the hope of guaranteeing that they would not vanish again.

Back at the dak bungalow I told Mr Kakpori of my strange encounter with the Minaro-speaking negotiator in the bazaar. Kakpori said that he knew the man, 'a Drok-pa from Garkund'. One of Kakpori's aides added confidentially, 'He's with army intelligence.'

Thus it was that this obliging intelligence officer sealed my fate with Sonam and Tashi, not without irony in view of my Machiavellian plan.

Finally we decided that we could not wait any longer for Nordrop and prepared to leave. I had begun to worry seriously about what could have become of my closest friend. I wondered if he had fallen ill, or perhaps set off on a long pilgrimage to a remote area. We had now waited in Kargil for nine days; it was already getting cold, and the willow trees were turning gold as they rustled in the cool, sharp autumn breezes.

The night before we left Kargil I went through our equipment one last time. There was no telling how long the journey would take, much less how it would end. We had therefore packed enough provisions for at least three weeks and all the camping gear we would need for crossing high passes. I was particularly concerned about Missy, whom I would have to abandon somewhere alone if Nordrop did not arrive, a situation that few women, in the best of circumstances, would have considered with any form of enthusiasm. Bad enough to be left alone in some strange valley, without the task of avoiding raising any kind of suspicion and patiently waiting for my safe return. 'Don't worry, I'll be fine,' Missy assured me with her characteristic good humour. I just prayed that she was right.

Hopeful that Nordrop might still turn up, I left instructions for him to join us at the Chamba whose inscription I was officially off to record.

Carefully I checked my special gear, my clothes appropriately 'aged' thanks to a good dose of old tea leaves, curry sauce and several sweepings across the dirty floor.

11

THE GOLD-DIGGING
ANTS

It was a fine, cold morning when at last we set off with our new friends Sonam and Tashi in a rented jeep. What a relief it was to get out of Kargil!

Turning up the Suru valley we left behind us the large army camp through which ran the strategic road. Few valleys in the Himalayas are as beautiful as the Suru, with its vast oasis-like fields hemmed in by stark mineral cliffs. Soon, on either side, appeared the towering heights of snow peaks and crumbling glaciers, the buttresses of the Zanskar range. On our way we passed the village of Trespon where I had once interviewed an artisan who still made the complex Scythian type of bows, still used by the Minaro. The true Minaro bows were made, in accordance with their taboo, entirely from ibex horns and sinews.

Leaving the Suru valley at the village of Sanku, we took to a rugged trail up a side valley which soon became a pitted mule track just this side of the village of Kartsé. Having unloaded a mile from the village, we bade goodbye to our driver and found ourselves on a steep ridge with Sonam and Tashi. There is always something tense in the atmosphere when one finds oneself, for the first time, alone with near strangers. We were now totally dependent on Sonam and Tashi, who were still quite unsuspecting as to what I had in store for them.

I went off to look for a suitable camp site, down a steep trail that led to a little irrigation canal which I followed until it passed beside a steep cliff face. Here, carved in the rock, stood the 28 foot tall figure of a Chamba, a massive standing Buddha, with thick lips and a slightly negroid face. As I looked up at it I noticed that it had been splattered with cow dung, thrown there, no doubt, as an insult by the local Muslim villagers.

I returned for the others and led the way while Sonam and Tashi brought down our equipment. We pitched camp beneath the Chamba. It was a small camp as we had only one tent with us and a couple of canvas sheets which we strung up to make a shelter for our two Minaro friends, Nordrop having kept our large mess tent in Zanskar.

I planned to stay for a day or two near the statue in the hope that Nordrop would join us. When camp had been settled I went out searching for wood with Sonam, in order to make a 10 foot ladder that would enable me to reach the level of the Buddha's thighs where the inscription was carved. A recent flash flood had uprooted some small trees by the riverside which made adequate poles for the makeshift ladder.

Sonam soon proved to be a willing, keen companion, offering at every moment to help around the camp. Tashi was equally agreeable, but much more reserved. They formed a truly odd couple, yet however strange they looked we could not help but feel a close tie with them, were it simply based on their European appearance. It was evident to them, as much as to us, that we were blood-brothers. We now began to appreciate how out of place they must have felt in a Mongolian world. Even the Aryan, dark-skinned Indian soldiers were alien to them. These Minaro, I realized, not only looked like Europeans but also had a similar temperament. As opposed to the gentle Mongolian-featured Zanskaris such as Nordrop, their manner was abrupt. Like ourselves they were excitable and extroverted, and more talkative than the Tibetans, Zanskaris or Ladakhis. They jumped up and moved around in a jerky manner that I now, for the first time, saw to be typical of Europeans. Their movements were somehow less deliberate and graceful than those of the Asiatics, while they commented aloud their intentions and thoughts in a manner quite alien to Orientals. Observing them I appreciated how, in the course of twenty-three years in the Himalayas, I had got so used to the Mongolian way of doing things that I now found the behaviour of these Minaro, so like our own, to be strange. At times Missy and I found ourselves addressing Sonam and Tashi in English, so hard was it to realize that they could not speak it.

Sonam was 33 years old and married to the wife of his elder brother. The custom of fraternal polyandry prevalent among the

Minaro is well expressed in their kinship terminology in which the word for mother, *aie*, is also used to describe a paternal uncle's wife. Such generalized polyandry points to a matriarchal society, although in the case of the Minaro inheritance goes to the males, never to the females. When a man dies his possessions go first to the eldest son, then to his father's elder or younger brother in that order, or if they are dead to the husband of the man's paternal aunt, or to the grandfather if he is the only surviving male heir.

Tashi, we learnt, had a baby daughter of 9 months, his first child by his elder brother's wife. 'You should see how beautiful she is,' he said proudly. We now began to appreciate that despite the startling ragged appearance of our two friends, their demeanour was not without dignity. Sonam was forever turning back his shirt cuffs and combing his hair, adjusting with the utmost seriousness his rather ridiculous woollen hat. Tashi likewise took great pains to keep his braids adjusted under an equally inappropriate looking bonnet.

It was evident that coming with us was a great adventure for them both. They marvelled at our equipment: the inflatable mattresses, the zips of our tent, our clothes, sleeping bags, camera and even scissors were minutely examined. They were most intrigued with our notebooks, volunteering any information we might need to clarify the abundant notes we had already gathered on the Minaro, such as the precise details of festivals and religious ceremonies. They told us about a spring festival in which all the inhabitants of Dartzig went up to their high pastures to live for two days in caves before offering juniper branches and flowers to the standing stone that marks the shrine of Basenden, the fairy goddess of pastures. They saw no conflict between their ancient beliefs and Buddhism, and indeed there was none, for the philosophical creed of Buddhism leaves place for ancillary deities.

Tashi was particularly pious, often mumbling prayers as he sat around our fire, studiously learning some of our strange culinary habits. We likewise watched in awe as he extracted goats' milk butter from a rather shady looking leather bag to add to his tea. There was a melancholy air about Tashi; whether this was concern for his long-awaited daughter or the sign of a man harassed by a difficult wife, we could not tell.

Both our friends ate very little, which explained their lean and hungry looks and lithe bodies. When I declared that I was 45 they thought me very old, and seemed a little puzzled that I should take such pains to travel this inhospitable land. I tried to explain to them some of the inventions of modern society, surprised at how few amounted to anything as extraordinary as I liked to imagine. They knew about aeroplanes, helicopters, cars and trucks, and had come across electricity in Kargil. What else could I add from the short list of technological marvels that compensate for the plagues of our industrial society? There was, of course, the tale of men on the moon, but that was hardly more startling than the Minaro's fairies who flew about at will, riding upon the beams of houses, on speaking terms with the rabbit they believed inhabited the moon; and anyway the achievements of NASA were hardly my own.

I had much more to say about French wine, and found that Sonam shared with me a sincere interest in the beverage of Diony-sus. Together we deplored the fact that at Kartsé the Muslims neither brewed *chang* nor made wine; we could hardly wait to reach Buddhist territory and feel the warmth that a good drink brings. While the two of them spoke longingly about the abundant grapes and apples back in their village, they plied us constantly with apricots they had brought along, dried in the sun, whose small kernels we also ate with relish. To make up for the lack of wine Sonam entertained us with songs about polo, with a cheerleader's dirge in Minaro, and other songs about beautiful girls.

Better than ever before, as we talked with these distant cousins, I understood that through the ages man had not changed. Only technology had altered, its accomplishments barely dissimulating the naïve, primitive creatures that we still are. Stone Age man, I now perceived, had been little different from us, perhaps more fortunate, subject to fewer strains than those imposed by our modern social and economic systems that make even the simplest rewards costly in hours of work that the Minaro would find degrading and futile.

As we sat that evening round our small fire we could hear, wafting over the valley, the staccato beat of working songs as men in single file, like walking hayricks, carried the harvest towards their houses. Under the enigmatic gaze of the giant Buddha we came to feel united in a bond of friendship. Fellow passengers upon the same whirling planet, here we had time to note the course of the sun and the creeping changes in atmosphere as night brought with it the fragrance of the freshly cut fields and the bitter tinge of eternal snows.

The following morning the first thing Sonam and Tashi did was to kneel and pay reverence to the Buddha. As soon as we had made our ladder they took great pains and some risks to dislodge the cow dung from the statue, often standing on one another's shoulders to do so.

All day long a stream of visitors came from the nearby village of Kartsé to see us. These people all had pronounced European features, a fact that was explained by the local belief that Kartsé had always been a Drok-pa settlement, its fortress having been founded by the same Minaro ruler who had governed Gyagam in Zanskar. The village itself was composed of a cluster of houses set beside a massive rectangular rock that soared 200 feet above the river. It was there that the fortress of Kartsé had stood, of which there was now no trace.

While we waited for Nordrop we occupied ourselves recording the ancient inscription that stood some ten feet off the ground to the left of the Buddha's right leg. Somehow both the statue and inscription seemed to have eluded the notice of most scholars. Francke mentions its existence, though he never saw it. Later travellers such as Skropski saw the statue but apparently missed the inscription. It is easy to see how this could have happened, for the Chamba's great size forces one to stand some distance back where the small characters of the 18 line inscription would be scarcely visible.

We spent many hours painstakingly copying the archaic Tibetan characters, photographing them at various hours of the day. These records, I hoped, would enable us later to decipher the text which my limited knowledge of literary Tibetan did not allow me to translate on the spot. In the end the inscription proved to be in such bad condition that all one could deduce was that it was from the tenth century. It mentioned a king but his name had been deliberately struck out. It was nevertheless of interest as one of the few very ancient inscriptions in Tibetan of the area.*

* I must thank here Mr Samten Karmay for his efforts in deciphering those portions that were legible.

This gigantic Buddha was somewhat similar to the one we had
seen at Mulbekh which had been carved in the eighth century, the
time of the arrival of the first Tibetans to this region, though
Buddhism had already been introduced to the area in the second
century through the missionary zeal of King Kanishka. The Minaro
(who had been Buddhists since before the arrival of the Tibetans)
particularly revered the local, pre-Lamaist shrines, especially at
Mulbekh and Phokar Dzong, a nearby cave which we planned to
visit on our way to the military highway.

After two days, having recorded the inscription and all but given
up on Nordrop, I decided to go ahead with my plans. Thus the four
of us prepared to set off up the Hang valley to cross the 15,760 foot
Rusi-la pass that led to the lower Sapi-la pass and thus into the
Shergol valley. This journey of some 50 miles across the Zanskar
range would bring us back again to the strategic road running from
Kargil to Leh.

It would be a rugged two-day climb over a pass as high as Mont
Blanc, over 6,500 feet up from Kartsé. It was imperative that I find a
pony for Missy, who was bravely struggling along to the creak of
her metal knee-braces. I made arrangements for a horse to be
waiting for her in a village we would pass through a few miles
upstream. I then hired a local Kartsé man and his donkey to help
carry our loads.

We left at dawn, the villagers already chanting in the fields as they
brought in the remainder of the barley harvest in enormous bundles
on their backs. The trail climbed along the left bank of the bounding
Hung River, passing through a series of small hamlets whose neat,
whitewashed houses were outlined by the dark frieze of brushwood
stacked on their roofs for winter. We moved quickly and quietly
through these villages, hoping to avoid the notice of any officials.
At midday we reached the place where we were to collect Missy's
horse. While the men made a fire for their salty tea, I searched in
vain for the horse and its owner. When I returned to our little camp I
learnt that Missy had found several rocks carved with ibex, tokens
of gratitude to Gyantse-Lhamo, the fairy goddess of chance and
good fortune. We certainly seemed to need it.

After lunch we attacked the flanks of the Rusi-la pass, entering a
deep gully that led us among boulders and rocks across a paltry

stream, Sonam helping Missy to cross the steep rocks. Only those who have themselves climbed up Himalyan passes can fully appreciate the uncanny way in which, bend after bend, the trail reveals ever more ridges to climb, each giving the illusion that it will be the last one before the summit. In all respects the Rusi-la was a mighty pass of the cruellest kind. Missy was soon in great difficulty, and my throbbing temples and sweat-filled eyes hardly left me enough energy to encourage her. More and more frequently we had to halt and rest.

At one such stop we were joined by a group of jovial women on their way to a high distant pasture, where for the summer months they lived in stone shelters attending their herds. They kindly helped Missy, holding her hands as we slowly covered several more miles before we saw, to our great joy, the outline of stone shelters in the distance, nestled on a slope that was almost totally devoid of any forage. We had been climbing for eight hours.

Darkness was falling as we finally stumbled into a herd of yaks and *dzos*, to be met by innumerable children rushing out from Stone Age dwellings to look at us. In the freezing cold and growing darkness I planted our tent upon the only flat piece of land available, the roof of one of the cattle shelters. There Missy lay down to rest while Sonam and I made a dinner of sorts over a smoky, yak-dung fire.

That night, as the wind pounded against the sides of our exposed tent, I lay awake thinking how enviable was the shelter of a cave. Comfort, I mused, is entirely relative to one's expectations. Beyond doubt, our Stone Age ancestors had been quite comfortable in their fur-lined dwellings. Their lives had been filled with the excitement of the chase, rewarded by orgies of roasted meat. There are no indications that our forefathers were in any way deprived of the essentials of life – indeed their daily fare included much of what we now consider luxuries, from snails to frogs' legs to fresh fruit and berries. It is ironic that today the rich in the West aspire to these very common delights of Stone Age men. Hunting and fishing are for us a luxury.

The following morning, when we arose to a breakfast of buttered tea and yoghurt, we found our tent covered in ice. My main concern now was for Missy. I had been promised a yak for her to ride to the still distant summit of the pass, and we were soon off looking for the elusive beast which we finally caught on a relatively flat ledge at the foot of the pass. The owner told us that she would not be coming with us, and that once we reached the summit we should just turn the yak round and chase it back down the pass. Having issued these instructions the owner then asked for thirty rupees, which I paid gladly enough while thinking that there could hardly be an easier way to make a little money.

With some difficulty Missy mounted our rather sleepy yak which began plodding upwards. As we climbed we encountered on the barren slopes, to our great amazement, little white flowers at the base of brittle, dry stalks of what seemed to be some sort of grass. It seems that during the night these strange plants exude water which quickly freezes into curly white ribbons that look like the peel of an apple. This forms a beautiful but fragile cluster of 'ice flowers' at the base of these plants. I had never before seen or even heard of such ice flowers and wondered if they were particular to this region. Awed, we watched them melt under the rising sun.

Puffing away, we reached the first snow fields and began an arduous traverse across rock slabs. Our yak seemed peaceful enough and quite sure-footed, though I did break Missy's stick on its back in an effort to keep it lumbering along. We were all exhausted when at last we reached the summit marked by a stone cairn in which were planted numerous branches festooned with prayer flags. This was a reminder that we were now entering Buddhist territory. All around us glistened an amazing array of snow-covered peaks. To the south we could see the distant Great Himalayan Range, to the north the mountains of Ladakh, while to the east and west rose the towering summits of the Zanskar range. On top of the pass Sonam pointed out the mountains behind which his village lay. They were many miles away but my heart beat with excitement as I took a first look at my secret goal. Would I be able to reach it? I had not yet dared broach the subject with our friends.

Having duly turned the yak round and chased it back down the pass with stones, we began to descend the steep scree slope that led to the distant headwaters of the Sapi-chu, a river that rose to the Sapi-la pass, which we hoped to cross the following day. The ridge along which we were walking forked and suddenly we were lost, although still in sight of our distant goal. Neither my Minaro companions nor the donkey owner had taken this route before and the snows of the previous severe winter had erased any semblance of a trail. Far beneath us to our right we spotted a herd of yaks, so I sent Tashi ahead to discover if that was where our route lay or whether we should instead descend down the left side of the steep ridge.

An hour later Tashi returned, having found no one to tell him the way. Stumbling down, uncertain of our route, we cut across scree slopes in what we hoped was a direct line for the Sapi River, which by now had disappeared from sight. It was to prove a long and harrowing descent which exhausted us all, particularly Missy who had to limp sideways down the steeper slopes. Watching her I began to doubt the sanity of this entire venture, and while I admired her courage I felt guilty for having made her embark, once again, on a venture that was not only physically too difficult for her but one that might soon prove hazardous in many other ways. I knew she was reaching the limit of her strength as, five hours after we had crossed the pass, we continued down the sheer walls of scree that fell nearly vertically into the Sapi River. We reached the river at dusk, just as a freezing wind began to rush up the valley. Removing our shoes we formed a human chain and slowly made our way across the icy stream, heading for the shelter of a vast rectangular house whose prayer flags fluttered in the strong wind.

Again we pitched our tent on a roof. Later, as we sat round another smoky, yak-dung fire with our host and our Minaro friends, I realized that the difficult march over the pass had sealed our friendship. It was time to tell them of my true intentions.

By now Sonam and Tashi were well aware of my special interest in the Minaro. They knew that over the years I had learnt a great many of their customs, collected a detailed vocabulary of their language and studied their religion. I now began to make discreet remarks about how very much I wished to go to their village. Sonam seemed enthusiastic and said that he would like me to meet his family. I left it at that as I made arrangements to hire a pony for Missy for the next day's journey over the Sapi-la.

The next morning we broke camp as soon as our host had produced a rugged Tibetan pony which he agreed to lead over the pass. The young woman of the house came to see us off wearing a magnificent *perak*, a turquoise-studded hat in the Mulbekh style with a wide leather strap that formed a long peak over her eyes. The entire strap was studded with her dowry, as is the local custom, and framed by two ear-like flaps of black, curly sheep's wool, similar to those of Zanskar.

As we struggled up the Sapi-la pass I went over my plan once again. It was my intention to descend into the valley on the opposite side and get as far as I could before coming upon the Muslim village of Shergol beside the military road. There we would camp and wait for a while in the hope that Nordrop would catch up with us.

After resting at the summit of the Sapi-la we made our way down into the deep valley that leads to Shergol. It took us several hours to reach the first villages clinging to the slopes, and these we passed as rapidly as possible, heading for the river's edge where we faced the sight of a major disaster. A few weeks earlier torrential rains, unusual for this barren area, had started a large mud slide that had swept down the valley, ripping out trees, destroying houses and killing cattle whose rotting carcasses lay half-buried in the now dry, caked mud. With great difficulty we picked our way across the chaos of trees and putrid bodies. It was nearing three o'clock when I caught sight, in the distance, of the bottom of the valley and the road beyond which no foreigners were allowed. Time had come, I felt, to seek a secluded place to camp.

We found the ideal spot, a little village called Sershing whose ten houses were huddled on both sides of a stream that emerged from two high cliffs. Here, away from the trail, we found an expanse of grass under some willow trees where we pitched our tent.

I still clung desperately to the hope that Nordrop might yet appear. I had by now mentioned his name so many times to Sonam and Tashi that they must have begun to think him a mythical creature. I was afraid that they might perhaps think I had made him up and might no longer trust me. Anyway that night, unable to postpone it any longer, I began to hint at my plans. In hesitant terms I explained that I very much wanted to go to their village, to Dartzig.

Sonam listened attentively and then remarked, 'Well, let's go back to Kargil and get a jeep!'

'No, no,' I exclaimed, 'I think it would be much better if we walked there.'

'But you must have a pass,' Tashi declared.

I was ready for this and explained that there was no problem, that Sheikh Abdullah had very much wanted me to go there because I was studying the land's *luço*, the Tibetan word for customs.

But then Sonam asked again, 'Why not take a jeep or bus down the road?'

I hastily changed the subject as I feared it was becoming obvious to Sonam and Tashi that there was something strange about my request. I heard them get into a rather heated argument out in the shadows as I remained near the fire.

'We shall stay here for a few days,' I called to them, bidding for time before I revealed the rest of my plan.

The next day, alas, there was still no sign of Nordrop, and I began to lose hope. His not showing up now seemed to worry my companions almost as much as it did me. No doubt they would have liked the presence of a monk who would vouch that I was indeed a good and honest person; for all they knew we might be crooks, since this was after all their first experience of foreigners.

We spent the following day resting and I took this opportunity to question my friends further about their traditions. Thus I learnt about their New Year festival, which in Dartzig features a race for boys under the age of nine, the winner receiving flowers. This custom recalls the New Year's race of naked children that was a tradition in Iran, the winner being named guardian of the Temple of the Sun. I already knew that the New Year in Minaro villages, as in Persia, was associated with fire.

That afternoon, seated around our smoky fire drinking salty tea, I questioned Sonam and Tashi about stories of ants or gold. They said they knew of no stories about gold-digging ants but added, 'Our fathers told us about collecting gold sand from the burrows of marmots.'

'What?' I exclaimed.

'Yes, the old people say they used to go to the plain of Dansar to collect gold sand from the marmot burrows, *phia ser nake liung* (gold-digging marmots). You see,' Sonam continued, 'the marmots bring up sand from underground and it has gold in it.'

I could hardly believe my ears. I made Sonam repeat the story twice. I then questioned Tashi. He confirmed the story, adding that the gold sand was no longer collected although this used to be a common practice in Dartzig.

'But where is the Dansar plain?' I asked excitedly.

'Between Ganosh and Morol,' came the reply. 'It's a dry, high plain, like a desert, with lots of marmots.'

The words of Herodotus suddenly came back to me:

There are other Indians further north, round the city of Kaspatyros and in the country of Pactyica, who in their mode of life resemble the Bactrians. These are the most warlike of the Indian tribes, and it is they who go out to fetch the gold – for in this region there is a sandy desert. There is found in this desert a kind of ant of great size – bigger than a fox, though not so big as a dog. Some specimens, which were caught there, are kept in the palace of the Persian kings. These creatures, as they burrow underground, throw up sand in heaps, just as our own ants throw up the earth, and they are very like ours in shape. The sand has a rich content of gold, and this it is that the Indians are after when they make their expeditions into the desert. . . . According to the Persians, most of the gold is got in the way I have described; they also mine a certain quantity – but not so much – within their own territory.

Thus it was, at long last and quite by accident, that I received the first confirmation that gold was collected from the sand dug up by these 'giant ants' as Herodotus, for lack of a better word, had called marmots. Everything matched the Greek story: the desert, the size of the 'ants', their fur as mentioned by Nearchos, and the people still called Darades by the Kashmiris! I rushed to tell Missy the news and then quickly rummaged through my kitbag for the maps. There I found, barely twenty miles west of Dartzig, the Ganosh valley and the small town of Morol on the edge of the Indus, just where the Suru and Shingo rivers united and joined the great river. There, right there, my friends confirmed, was the *thang* or plain of Dansar, the exact location of the land of the gold-digging marmots, creatures that 'as they burrow underground throw up sand in heaps, just as our ants throw up the earth.'

Herodotus had been right; he was not the liar that modern scholars had believed him to be, his story was far from being 'an extravagance . . . a remarkable tall one', as claimed by Professor A. R. Burns of Glasgow University. Herodotus had indeed reported the truth, and in some detail: 'gold is found here in immense quantity, either mined, or washed down by rivers, or stolen from the ants.' Gold was, I knew, washed down the Zanskar and Suru rivers, and also mined, as I had seen, a little further up the Indus from the plain of Dansar.

Why then had no one ever found this land, why had explorers, generals and scholars alike failed to discover the ants and their gold, allowing the story to grow and grow until it became one of the most fabulous legends of antiquity and later times? Why had Herrmann, the German scholar, or the Rev. Francke who spent so many years in Ladakh, not found the origin of this legend?

The answer was simple, written there upon my map, spelt out on the faces of my Minaro companions, explained by the jagged peaks that surrounded us. The land of the gold-digging ants, the Dansar plain and the area immediately surrounding it was, and still is, one of the most inaccessible of our entire planet. That is why even Francke it seems never visited the villages south of Dartzig where for thousands of years the origin of the ants' gold had been kept secret.

It is no coincidence that the Minaro in the vicinity of the gold have survived unspoilt as the last, not lost Aryans in Tibet. Nor is it a coincidence that, as I now noticed on my map, the cease-fire line runs straight alongside the Dansar plain which in fact lies on the Pakistani side of the line. No coincidence, for it was, and still is, impossible for an invading army to penetrate this sanctuary. If Pakistani and Indian troops had stopped on either side of this plain it was because neither could wage war in the natural rat-traps formed by the valleys of the surviving Minaro, valleys like those of Ganosh and Dartzig, and those of Dah, Hanu and Garkund which fell nearly vertically from 17,000 foot high passes into the vertical walled trough of the Indus gorge. To enter these short, steep valleys would be military suicide. Here the Minaro had survived, captives of their own vales, molested neither by the invading armies of the kings of

Tibet nor by those of the Muslim warlords who had waged war in the adjacent areas for hundreds of years; undisturbed too by passing travellers, for the trade route which elsewhere followed the Indus was here forced to scramble out of the river's gorge. It was indeed no coincidence that the plain of the gold-digging marmots had escaped discovery for centuries, for this area had always remained just beyond the extreme limits of all the Old World's great empires: the only one ever to have effectively ruled this area was the great Persian Empire of Darius in the fifth century BC. And that is how the story of the ants' gold came to be known; for Herodotus got his account from Persian soldiers who had seen marmots in their king's palace.

What was later to deceive researchers in their quests for this gold was the manner in which Herodotus wrote about it. Two aspects of his account were misleading: first was his use of the word ant to describe what was, in all evidence, a marmot; second was his claim that these 'ants' were dangerous. To his credit it must be said that Herodotus used the term ant with caution, and only for lack of a better analogy, stating that the 'creatures' brought up the gold-bearing sands in the manner of ants bringing up earth.

Curiously enough most recent scholars, Herrmann, Laufer and Francke, to name a few, had remained fixed on ants rather than trying to identify the creatures in question. There were, though, a few exceptions. C. Ritter, in 1833, was the first person to suggest that they might be marmots, but then he ignored all the indications as to the geographical location of the ants' gold being the Land of the Dards. Ritter thought that the land of the gold-digging marmots might be at the source of the Sutledge River near the sacred peak of Kalash, basing this on Moorcroft's report that both marmots and gold were to be found in the area (although Moorcroft never linked the two, nor did any local account).

Herrmann, on the other hand, writing in 1938, correctly identi-fied the area referred to by Herodotus as the Land of the Dards, a land not far from Kashmir, although at that time the Dards' true home, as we have seen, had not been precisely identified. But Herrmann, like others, discarded marmots, preferring to believe in ants. His reason for doing so was that he was particularly struck by the ferocity of the 'ants' mentioned by Herodotus, knowing that marmots are generally considered tame. (This is not entirely true, since they will fiercely defend themselves if their burrows are attacked.) It was indeed misleading that both Herodotus and Megasthenes went to great pains to explain how aggressive the ants were and how, therefore, one had to steal the gold in great haste. It now appeared evident to me that these tales were the normal complement to every story about hidden treasure and riches; not only did they offer a natural explanation as to why the treasure had not been located or stolen, they might also have been spread specifically to discourage adventurers from seeking it.

There could be little doubt that what Sonam and Tashi had told me was at the root of the myth of the ants' gold. The ants were marmots, the large Asiatic marmot known as *Arctomys himalayas,* a marmot with a long bushy tail like that of a fox, found only in high, desolate valleys or plains above 12,000 feet, which corresponds to the height of the Dansar Plain. (The Tibetan word for plain, *thang*, applies to any flat plateau, however small. If Herodotus misleadingly mentions a desert, this is no doubt because of the sandy nature of the place, while Megasthenes correctly reports it as a mountain plateau.) Marmots, being hibernating animals, dig vast and complex barrows, throwing up at the entrances great mounds of earth three or more feet high, which may cover an area over ten yards square. This sand, were it gold-bearing, would certainly yield, after being sifted, sufficient gold to make it worthwhile stealing, and this is exactly what the men of Dartzig did.

It would be no great stretch of the imagination to say, as claimed by Nearchus, that the marmots' fur, being dark brown, red and beige, was like that of a panther – the clouded rather than the spotted variety. Moreover, Himalayan marmots are truly bigger than foxes and yet, being very close to the ground, smaller than most dogs, as Herodotus had claimed. Interestingly Herodotus uses the word *Murmex* for ant: this might once have described both ant and marmot.

There could be no doubt that what Sonam and Tashi had told me was at the root of the myth of the ants' gold. I now had evidence to show that the region was inhabited by people the Kashmiris called the Darades, the same name used by Megasthenes who, we must remember, got his information while in India, no doubt from Kashmiris.

In considering how and why the identity of the Dansar Plain and its gold-digging marmots escaped notice for so long, one must mention the language problem. Minaro, as understood by the local people, is one of the most obscure, ill-known and least-spoken languages of Asia. The only other language the Minaro can understand is archaic Tibetan, spoken by very few foreigners. Fluent as I was in Tibetan, it had taken me fully three years in the area to elicit, from friends, this well-guarded secret.

The excitement of this discovery made me, for a while, forget the anxiety surrounding my proposed mission. That evening with Sonam I crossed the small river to a neighbouring house where three old hags brewed excellent *chang*. It was cold and very late when, slightly drunk, we stumbled back in the dark together towards our tents.

12

IN DISGUISE

The discovery of the location of the gold, later confirmed by other inhabitants of Dartzig, only reaffirmed my resolve to enter into the forbidden zone, were it only for a day, to look upon the land of the Minaro and the plain of the gold-digging marmots. My mind was made up. I would wait no longer for Nordrop. But how to seduce my two friends into accompanying me? They knew well that their land was forbidden to all foreigners, and they also knew the power of the Indian army, its police and implacable laws. They were simple fellows, but with enough common sense not to want to take any risks for a foreigner, even one whom they knew to be a friend of their people.

Thinking all this over, I realized that the only way I could get them to lead me across the inner line was by trickery. I would have to deceive them. This worried me a great deal because living with them over the past days, toiling up passes, sharing our meals and shivering side by side, we had become true friends.

I had on the other hand fewer qualms about deceiving Indian officials and bureaucrats and felt that I should carry on before time could obliterate for ever the collective memory of the Minaro. In twenty-three years of exploration and study in the Himalayas I had received little but rebuttals from the Indian government and its agents. They had bantered with my time and money, seeking, at best, bribes and generally paying me with scorn and indifference.

I now made my intentions clear to Sonam and Tashi, telling them that I already had the necessary permit and the backing of many powerful officials and that there would be no problems. I was, I admit, ashamed about this lie. Sonam seemed confident that everything would be all right, but older and wiser Tashi seemed suspicious and, I feared, smelt a rat. They discussed the matter between themselves for some time. What was going on, I could not tell. Certainly they must have seen me as some sort of scholar, or perhaps a 'lama from the West' who read holy inscriptions and paid reverence to Lord Buddha. Not waiting for a reply, I took out my map and showed them the route I wished to take. I pointed out the trail that ran from the little village of Lotsum up to a pass called the Bu-la. This pass led down to the road that the army had blasted into Minaro territory, which crossed the same range over the Hamboting-la to the other side of the mountain. Through delicately phrased questions I discovered that beside the Bu-la there was another pass, the Shashi-la, that led to a ridge from which I should be able to see Dartzig and the Dansar plain.

If we took this route up to the Shashi-la, to the head of the Dartzig valley, I would at long last be able to see and tread upon the soil of the land of the Minaro – that is if I could elude the military and the police in the village of Lotsum, and whatever other check-posts and patrols there might be in the villages along the river that led from Lotsum up the pass into Minaro territory.

I now explained this plan in detail to Sonam, who asked me directly, 'But what if the police stop you?'

'That's all right. I have my pass, and furthermore I have a lot of connections. Was it not a government official, a Minaro, who negotiated for your salary? Everything will be all right; there's nothing to worry about. But still,' I added, 'it would be best if no one noticed me, so I have brought along some clothes to make me look like a Minaro. It will be easier that way.' I showed him my clothes and wrapped my shawl around me. I dared not yet disclose that I would dye my skin and hair.

Sonam seemed to buy my story, but once again the two went off to confer.

A little while later they came back and Sonam said to me, eyeing Tashi nervously, 'Are you sure there won't be any trouble? There are soldiers stationed in Dartzig to guard the bridge over the Indus and they are always stopping people and causing trouble.' It was obvious that they were getting nervous about the whole idea again. I decided to talk later privately with Tashi and try to allay his fears. However well I had mastered Tibetan, it was not easy to make myself perfectly clear as my friends spoke a Balti cum Ladakhi-Tibetan dialect whose archaic pronounciation differed from Tibetan, making some of my words difficult for them to understand. Tashi explained clearly that it was out of the question for me to go right into their village and that he did not want any part in the plan. Fearing that all might be lost I quickly changed the subject. 'Let's have a drink,' I suggested and led my friends back across the river to the old hags' house for some more of their good *chang*.

The following morning, nursing a slight hangover, I noticed that a few hundred yards from where we were camping was a long, narrow, grassy strip, the village polo ground. The strip was some forty paces wide and nearly three hundred long, lined on both sides by a short, stone wall. I was told that in 1980 His Holiness the Dalai Lama had held a religious service in this very village, preaching from a throne set up by the polo field. Tashi explained this to me with great reverence, telling me how he, along with many other Minaro, had come here to hear His Holiness. The village was just below the holy shrine known as Urgyen Phokar Dzong, 'the white cave fortress of Urgyen'. Urgyen, known also as Guru Rimpoche, was the monk (now a saint) who introduced Buddhism into Tibet in the eighth century, coming here from Swat. This shrine is one of the holiest and oldest in the area and was chosen by the Dalai Lama for his place of meditation on his tour of Ladakh. From Sershing he had gone for a retreat of several days at Phokar Dzong.

Playing for time in the hope of persuading Sonam and Tashi to take me into their valley, and still not having given up all hope of Nordrop arriving to keep Missy company, I decided to take my friends to Phokar Dzong. When Sonam explained how difficult the route was I decided that Missy should stay in camp.

The trail we took led us to the entrance of a narrow, rock-enclosed gorge. Here we found several isolated carvings of ibex before coming across an entire cliff face covered with them. Leaving these familiar signs of Minaro worship, we began to climb up the canyon and were soon forced to walk in the stream that bounced down in a gully only three feet wide between two immense rock faces which in places obscured the sky.

We climbed for two and a half hours before emerging upon a

ridge encircled by towering cliffs; we had reached the holy shrine, announced by a modern rectangular whitewashed chapel, the one in which the Dalai Lama had stayed. In front of the chapel rose two newly built, rectangular *chortens*, topped with a cluster of juniper branches and handsome, curved horns of ibex. These were Buddhist monuments built for the arrival of the Dalai Lama, shrines to Lamaist divinities. I now looked at them for what they truly were, shrines to Gyantse-Lhamo and Shiringmen-Lhamo, the original fairy goddesses of the ancient Minaro cult. Kneeling and touching the holy ground the ritual three times with their foreheads, Sonam and Tashi made their devotions before these shrines.

From the ridge beside the chapel we looked out over a deep chasm to a huge cliff, pierced with caves. It was in one of these caves that Guru Rimpoche, the Father of Lamaism, had meditated. He it was who had brought Buddhism to Tibet, a monk whose genius was in allowing local, native beliefs to be incorporated into Buddhism. Around the foot of the cave stood a dozen huge, gnarled juniper trees, the sacred tree of Stone Age worship which, if cut, could cause death.

At the time we came to Phokar Dzong a very holy lama was meditating in Guru Rimpoche's cave. Another monk, a servant of the lama, told us that he would spend a total of three months in solitary meditation. My friends were overjoyed, not only to be at one of their holiest shrines, but also to be in close proximity to such a venerable lama. With them I visited the other unoccupied caves and a cavern in which two small *chortens* stood. A resident monk began scraping out earth from the walls of the cavern; this he gave to Sonam and Tashi who, to my amazement, began to eat it. Upon their repeated insistence I also tasted some of the holy earth. To my surprise I found it light and crumbly, and not totally indigestible. Apparently Guru Rimpoche had lived solely upon this sacred soil and those who imitated him would be blessed.

We then went to the lama's assistant, whom Tashi asked for a special blessing on his baby daughter. This monk began to chant prayers and presented us with holy strands of red and blue silk cord which we were to tie round our necks. I was fascinated by the whole procedure, and with my holy strand around my neck I continued to examine with care the rest of the caves.

Sonam and Tashi, no doubt impressed by my conversation with the lama's assistant, unexpectedly announced that they had taken counsel and that as they were sure I was a good man they would now take me to their land. I dared not believe my ears. I realized that it was this visit to Phokar Dzong that had sealed my fate, for blessed and approved by the monks, and having shown great reverence for their religion, I was no longer suspect. Sonam and Tashi had decided to respect and fulfil my wishes.

Although I had lied to them, about which I still felt a certain remorse, I began to feel that perhaps this was all Buddha's will. Had I not, for years, studied with reverence all things Buddhist, and although not a Buddhist myself I could see that perhaps I did deserve from this religion of tolerance the endorsement of my project by the very people I cherished. The 'sin' I was about to commit was solely one against the modern government in Delhi. Maybe it was fitting that, in the end, it was my companions' faith that was to allow me to carry out my plan.

Back at the camp with Missy we began our final preparations in earnest. To allay any residual fear my companions might still have, I showed them an official document which I said was my permit. This deliberate lie on my part would exonerate them of any responsibility, so that if I were caught, I should be solely responsible for abusing the goodwill of these simple, illiterate men.

Although this made me feel somewhat better I still had to consider the risks that I was about to take. Under no circumstances must I allow myself to be caught, which meant that I would have to slip unnoticed past all police and military checkposts. To do this I felt that it was imperative to travel by night, but how could I explain this to my friends without once more arousing their suspicions?

With Missy I invented the excuse that she would be staying behind because of her bad knees, and also to wait in case Nordrop came. Sonam and Tashi accepted this arrangement without question. Missy didn't seem to mind staying behind in camp, especially as we were now friendly with most of the villagers who had agreed to help keep her supplied with twigs and yak dung for her fires. She would wait it out alone in Sershing until I returned, or she learnt of my capture. It is a fact that crime is virtually unknown in Ladakh, but I admired Missy's courage. Although she was far from helpless she was partially handicapped in this land, the sight of which would make her doctor wince, and her Tibetan vocabulary was limited. She fully appreciated the risks we were both running, and that this journey could end in prison. But by now we had spent so much time, passion and energy in pursuit of our goal that it was out of the question to turn back. I was only sad that Missy could not share with me this final stage in our long, mutual quest for the identity of the Dards and the land of the gold-digging ants.

While Sonam, Tashi and I were away at the Phokar Dzong Missy had brewed the walnut peels to make the dye for my skin. The following morning I went with her to the riverside to prepare my make-up. By now I was becoming almost paranoid, telling Missy to hide everything each time I heard a twig break. Between furtive glances I rubbed my face, chest and hands with Missy's brew until I had taken on a golden hue, which I enhanced by smearing dirt all over myself. Missy then proceeded to dye my hair and eyebrows dark brown, using the toothbrush we had brought for this purpose.

Back in camp I put on my long Pakistani shirt and grubby local sweater, tucking them into my own mountain trousers. Until we reached the strategic road I was not going to take any chances of being caught in disguise. My rough shepherd's shawl, baggy trousers and woolen cap I packed into an old sack that Sonam would carry as far as the strategic road where, to complete my disguise, I would change and then carry the sack myself with a strap over my forehead to look more like my companions.

It was agreed that I should set out ahead on my own, as I did not want anyone to see us all leave camp together and so signal that Missy was alone. This suited my plans, for I could push on and reach Lotsum first and thus stop Sonam and Tashi from crossing the village before nightfall.

A little after noon I set off, in such a state of nervous anticipation that I forgot to hug Missy goodbye. Returning, I did this with an emotion I need not describe.

I walked for about two miles, following an irrigation canal that rose above the main trail down the valley. From this vantage point I was soon able to see behind me the gangly silhouettes of Sonam and Tashi, carrying their belongings and my small bag. Keeping in sight of each other we continued, passing the foot of an amazing cliff monastery that rises right above the village of Shergol, a Muslim community with a minute mosque. As I walked I was filled with nervous excitement, becoming more and more suspicious of everything that moved and jumping at the sight of every pony, sheep or truck that I saw on the metalled highway below me.

When I reached the highway I knew that there was no turning back. At last I was living a real adventure of the kind I had longed for as a child. But this was no longer a game. The road was suddenly empty and it was of some comfort that I could still see the distant figures of my companions behind me. This was the beginning of a three-hour walk in which every encounter would be significant. What if a truck stopped to offer me a ride, or worse still a jeep full of government officials or Border Security Forces? I envisaged countless scenarios, practising the excuses for each one. I had nothing to worry about, I kept telling myself. 'I have every right to be on this road' – the road being the boundary north of which foreigners might not travel.

After an hour of meeting no one, I finally passed a Ladakhi on a pony and we exchanged *julays*, the traditional Ladakhi greeting. Soon I lost sight of Sonam and Tashi, and began to worry even more. What if they had turned back and abandoned me? As I walked along, lost in speculation, I rounded a bend and almost bumped into a parked truck, its Sikh driver busy drinking from a little rivulet. I feigned not to notice him and increased my pace. I had not gone far when I saw ahead of me on my right the tops of trees, which came into view as I neared a little village of mud-coloured huts, set in recently harvested barley fields. I stopped to ask an old woman how far was Lotsum, my destination. 'A few hours on,' she said vaguely. I left it at that and walked on like an automaton for another hour. It was getting cold and although I had been walking for only two hours I felt tired, or rather weary, or was it lonely? The tarmac rang hard against my old walking shoes, which in the end I decided would be much more comfortable on the long march than the new gym shoes I had bought in Kargil, and which were certainly shoddy enough to belong to a Minaro.

As I walked my thoughts turned to all the times I had travelled alone in the Himalayas, across the barren expanse of Mustang and then up the deep, dark and frightening wooded mountains of inner Bhutan. For more than half my life the Himalayas had been my second home, a place filled with faces, with memories of the friends, porters, cooks, monks and traders with whom I had shared the hardships of the trail: endless paths worn smooth by bare feet, or boots, or by the hoofs of countless cattle, ponderous yaks, trepidating goats and high-stepping ponies. These trails were eternal, the links not only from place to place, but with time. On similar trails had trodden the pilgrims of old, Marco Polo and the troops of Alexander. How ironic that now the trail of this adventure should begin as an ugly black tarmac smear across the landscape. No wonder Buddhist monks in Tibet and the Himalayas considered the blasting for a modern road to be a sin.

Soon I passed another village, and then a few lone houses clinging to a ledge above the Waka River. The rumbling of a truck pulled me out of my dreams. I turned my face from the driver's as the truck rushed by with its brute force, a creaking monster of our modern technology. Still lost in thought, I advanced to the rhythmic thud of my shoes for yet another hour. I must be getting near, I thought. My map was too general to have listed all the small villages, and anyway I had decided to leave it behind along with the small camera. At the last minute I had decided that it would be too risky to take either, since these more than anything might have branded me as a spy.

Still lost in thought I rounded a bend and ran into a young man. He eyed me with what I thought was suspicion. Immediately I asked him where Lotsum was. 'Far yet,' he answered in Ladakhi, then stopped in his tracks, surprised that I had spoken his tongue.

I was now very nervous. Where was this wretched village, how would I even recognize it? Soon I saw more trees and came upon another village. Was this it, I wondered, slowing down. No, this village was too small. I knew, or at least imagined I knew, what Lotsum should look like, set as it was on my map at the head of a long valley that led ultimately to the summit of the mountains that now separated me from the Indus. It must, I thought, be quite a large place. I had taken this road before on my way from Kargil to

Mulbekh and Leh, but of course had not then paid attention to Lotsum, a village whose very name now sounded ominous, conjuring up visions of checkposts and police. I now passed through a narrow gorge whose light ochre cliffs had been blasted away for the road. 'You can't miss Lotsum,' I remembered being told; 'there is a small bazaar there.' How small, I wondered, plodding along, perspiring in spite of the cold wind.

It was a little after three-thirty when, having passed a couple of fields still deep in thought, I rounded a large rock to find myself suddenly in full view of a village barely a hundred yards away. To my horror, I saw on the road before me a parked, khaki-coloured jeep. Beside the jeep were several low buildings, the shops of a bazaar. I stopped dead in my tracks. This was surely Lotsum; I had gone too far. I now saw, coming up the road, a large truck. Hastily I moved back behind the rock. What if the police or some checkpost officials had already seen me? I was really frightened. I turned round and walked back for half a mile before desperately searching for a place where I could hide and await my friends. This proved unnecessary as I soon caught sight of them advancing with their swingy, elastic gaits, Sonam draped in his burgundy red, home-spun wool gown that seemed far too short, and Tashi in an old polyester jacket that was much too big for him. They made a really strange-looking pair. I waved discreetly to them and walked across a stubble field, then down an embankment to the edge of the river. Sonam and Tashi scrambled down behind me.

'Let's make tea,' I said, finding a place behind a large boulder that protected us from the freezing wind. It was only a quarter to four.

Tashi began scrounging for dead branches. Suddenly a woman appeared, seemingly from out of nowhere, dressed in black with a veil hanging loosely over her face. She was, we gathered, the owner of the field above us, and began asking us the usual questions: 'Where are you from? Where are you going?' I told her we were on our way from Shergol to Kargil. Fortunately she soon wandered away, by which time we had a fire going.

I was exhausted with worry. I knew that now I would have to lay my cards on the table and explain to Sonam and Tashi that we should only travel at night. 'We had better wait to cross Lotsum,' I said nervously. 'No one ever knows with Indian officials.' They did not seem to understand. We drank our tea with goats' butter. I had packed no special provisions for myself. I would eat what they ate: tsampa (dry roasted barley), buttered tea, chapatis (unleavened wheat bread) and a few of the left-over apricots. I took my time munching several of these. I then looked at my watch; it was four-thirty. I had miscalculated badly. We had arrived at Lotsum far too early.

After cleaning up Tashi stood and said, 'Well, let's go.'

'No, no,' I heard myself saying, 'it's better if we don't run into the police.'

Tashi said nothing but began to speak to Sonam in Minaro. This I knew to be the crucial moment. Now or very soon they might realize that I had lied to them, that perhaps there was something wrong with the permit I had shown them. There was no way of telling what their reaction might be. They said nothing.

I had calculated that it would be dark by half-past six, which gave us a little more than an hour and a half to wait. Never in my entire life has time gone more slowly. Never has the sun seemed like such a permanent fixture, making no progress across the horizon, hidden as it was by the mountain that rose beyond the rushing river. Our fire was out and it was getting very cold. I extracted from my bag the thick woollen shawl I had brought along. It was crude, of poorly carded goats' hair, the colour of a dirty sheep. I wrapped it round me and put on my beige woollen Balti hat. At six o'clock it still seemed as light as ever.

'Let's go,' Tashi said again.

'No, we must wait,' I replied.

Tashi was visibly nervous. He was forever getting up and going to pee downstream; I must admit that I kept doing the same.

'What time is it?' asked Sonam.

'Quarter-past six,' I said, removing my watch and hiding it in my pocket.

'Let's make some more tea,' I suggested.

It seemed like a good idea. We soon had our fire roaring once more. Sonam fetched some water, and produced a chapati from the stack we had brought. I was trembling as I ate. It tasted terrible, or rather, it didn't taste of anything at all. I thought of Missy back there in Sershing. What if someone bothered her? I had urged her to move into a village house where she would be looked after, but she said she preferred to be by herself in the tent. Was I mad to have left her there alone?

Clouds appeared as it finally began to get dark. Six-thirty; maybe my watch was slow or had stopped. Tashi kept pacing up and down. 'Can you sing?' I asked Sonam, and soon he was humming a lively tune that he accentuated with clicking sounds and occasional slaps on his knees. I laughed nervously and sat down. It was almost dark and the clouds were passing slowly by. I now opened my bag and brought out my baggy Pakistani pants, putting them on over my mountain trousers and pulling out my long shirt tails to complete my disguise. But would I fool anyone? My companions looked at me and smiled.

I got up and stretched my hand out in front of me to see if I could still see the hairs on the back of my hand, which is how one established nightfall in Nepal. It was ten to seven. We got up. We were ready to go.

13

THE LOST HORIZON

Sonam led the way back to the road; I stumbled behind him, and Tashi followed me. We now walked in single file. I carried my near empty sack, keeping my hands close to my face while holding its strap. Everything now fell into place as I began my slouching Minaro walk, following Sonam blindly. I was too frightened to look around as we passed the stalls of the small bazaar on our right. The pale glow of kerosene wicks flicked from the houses. We turned off the road down a little path, past a house whose door was open. I bumped into a cow, then hurried on to catch up with Sonam.

Walking at a brisk pace we passed the shadows of several more houses, and rapidly started climbing a steep incline. We reached a little knoll. Blinking in the dark I could hardly discern the trail, and the only sound I heard was that of my breathing and fast pumping heart. I plodded on, hard on the heels of Sonam.

I was keenly alert, carefully minding where I put each foot, when I bumped into a wall, tripped and fell against Sonam who, for some reason, had stepped back suddenly. Then I heard a low growl and a man's voice. Tashi was now right behind me, holding on to my arm. Somehow we had stumbled on to the flat roof of a house whose owner was visibly angered. My heart pounded; I began to run behind Tashi, with Sonam close behind. We slithered down a slope and by some lucky chance managed to find the trail again. My eyes had now somewhat adjusted to the darkness and I realized that the village of Lotsum extended some way up the narrow valley in which we now found ourselves; houses, or rather the yellow flicker of their lights, were visible above us as we walked along the edge of an embankment, probably above terraced fields. Sonam, who had once more taken the lead, turned to indicate that we should be particularly quiet. On tiptoe was passed several houses, brushing their walls, past closed doors through which we occasionally caught a glimpse of light. I was congratulating myself on our safe passage alongside these dwellings when the ground suddenly gave way under me and I fell with what sounded like a thunderous crash. I had overstepped the trail and now found myself about three yards down in a field. Sonam and Tashi helped me up once again, and we carried on. I strained my eyes to see the trail, visible at times as a white line, at other times disappearing as my eyes blurred with fatigue. We had been walking for about an hour, and although I now began to relax a little, I felt weary. My mind began to wander. Was this not the most exciting moment of my entire life? I recalled my other adventures: my brush with the Khamba guerrillas in Mustang; the awesome loneliness of the trails in Bhutan which I had crossed in thirty-one days of painful, solitary travel. I remembered getting lost on glaciers in the main Himalayan range, with the dangers of the crevasses; all those hundreds, no thousands of miles I had paced in the most remote areas of the globe; and my first solitary journey down the coast of Quintana Roo, my only companions the occasional *chicleros* from the penal colony. But all this paled in comparison to this mission, behind which loomed the immense menace of an entire army. This was, I knew, forbidden territory. I had chosen to violate a law which had been more than clearly spelt out to me. I had been refused access to this area, and here I was.

'*Julay!*' The simple greeting made me start. Before I knew it I was looking into the faces of a man and an older woman who had come down in the trail towards us, unnoticed. As I turned away, Sonam began talking to them. They continued talking for what seemed like hours, and then we walked on. I sighed with relief. The man had a torch but apparently did not find me suspicious. What if it had been a patrol, or a police officer?

We were now well past Lotsum but were far from safe, for according to my map we had to cross four more villages before reaching the valley leading to the Shashi-la pass; villages through which we would have to pass without being seen. What about dogs, I wondered, remembering the ferocious Tibetan mastiffs kept by many local people: great burly animals, chained for life, who lunged at every passer-by. What also of those few dogs that were set loose at night?

Our next obstacle was to pass safely the village of Tatsa which, I had been told, contained a police station. I reckoned it was about ten miles ahead. I pulled my watch out of my pocket; it was eight o'clock. How much further would we have to walk before taking a rest, I wondered. I was bitterly cold, although I was perspiring heavily. Low clouds moved quickly across the very small crescent of the moon, creating eerie, ever-changing shadows. When we were under the trees that bordered the river I could see nothing at all; at other times the trail seemed populated by ghosts, the shadows of the rock sentinels that rose on either side of us. It was now 23 September, late, very late in the season. In less than a month heavy snow would close down the pass to Srinagar. Perhaps we should not have lost so much time in Pakistan, I worried; perhaps we should have come in spring?

We had been walking for what seemed a long time when we suddenly descended a steep slope and crossed a small stream in which I soaked my shoes. On the other bank I squelched up across several terraced fields, fearing that there must be a house near by. Sonam made signs for me to stop. Tashi, who had been bringing up the rear, went on ahead, coming back in a few minutes to talk to Sonam in a hushed voice. I gathered that we were lost. Looking around I realized that the valley had branched in two.

'Are you sure this is the trail?' I asked Sonam.

'No,' came his dismal reply.

For a moment I had a vision of us continuing down a wrong trail and ending up lost in some ravine. Tashi soon indicated that we should continue down the eastern branch of the valley and we clambered up the terraced fields until we found a little path, one that seemed much too small to be the right one. This we followed for about half an hour until Tashi, who was still in the lead, stopped and sat down. He was calling a rest. By now I was covered with perspiration. Taking my watch out I saw that it was only nine o'clock.

'Where shall we stop for the night?' I asked in a hushed voice.

'Not yet, not yet, we must first pass the police post at Tatsa.'

It was evident that Tashi wanted to push on and I did not blame him. A few short minutes later we struggled to our feet.

I had never walked any great distance at night before and now felt as if I were struggling in a cocoon of darkness, continually trying to rivet my eyes on Tashi's pale, bare heels where they emerged from his tattered, second-hand, plastic shoes. His moving feet were now my only guide. I could no longer see the trail and had to trust in where he trod, breathing down his neck, knowing that one false step could lead me over a precipice, as we were now quite high above the river. I began to marvel that I did not stumble more frequently, surprised at my own surefootedness. At times I felt that my feet had eyes of their own as I managed to stride on in uneven, rocky places. It was certainly my feet, much more than my eyes, that were guiding me, telling me what were loose rocks and what were rolling stones, taking an even keel to maintain my balance, quick to jump if the gravel began to slip, somehow finding foot-holds where I could perceive nothing but a blurred strip, slightly paler than the two dark borders.

A little further on we had to cross the stream again. As I bent down trying to find the stepping stones my hat fell in the water. I managed to rescue it, though it now weighed a ton. I wrung it out and put it back on my freezing head, but it plagued me as we carried on down what I feared might be the wrong trail. The village of Tatsa lurked in my mind with the image of a police officer sitting up late in front of his station alongside our trail.

Tatsa was now the focus of our attention; beyond Tatsa we could stop and rest. But we never seemed to reach it. The trail went up and up, and an hour later I feared that we had taken the wrong valley. All around us seemed desolate, and the rocks beneath my wet feet were very hard. We now heard a distant roar that signalled rapids and cascades. As we rose above the river I had to be even more careful where I put my feet. Occasionally Tashi would turn to give me a hand or to point out the broken edge of the precipice, indicating that I should hug the rock face. On one occasion Sonam fell down flat behind me. Progress was very slow, but mercifully the trail soon flattened out.

We had brought a torch but so far had not used it, both to spare the batteries for possible later emergencies and for fear of giving ourselves away. Now for occasional brief instants Tashi would flash it on, as if trying to determine which way to go. The light would blind me for the next five or so paces until once again I could perceive the vague contours of the trail, the ribbon of light set in pitch darkness which, for all I knew, could and often did have sheer drops on either side.

We could not be far from Tatsa now, I hoped. The trail, although not steep, hugged the river, but somehow it seemed we had lost it. I stood still while Sonam consulted in hushed tones with Tashi, who had become our leader. The older man seemed better able to follow the trail, although this ability did not seem to be much in evidence just now. Soon the cause of our problems became evident. As had happened in the Shergol valley, but here to a lesser degree, torrential rains had swept downriver a muddy flood which had washed away parts of the trail. In its wake the flood had left what was now bone dry, pockmarked clay with here and there deep footprints in which I kept twisting my ankles. We had already crossed the deep, bubbling black water of the stream several times, and I began to see our progress as a true miracle, unaware of what was yet to come. We were now, by all evidence, nearing Tatsa and had to stop using the torch.

As we plodded on up the tree-lined river, making slow progress in the near total darkness, I began to notice that on either side of us rose what seemed to be walls. I was straining to see where to put my feet next when I suddenly realized that Tashi was running in front of me. He had seen or heard something. I began to panic. Sonam was furtively searching for a way out from the stream, now fenced in on both sides. I saw before me the silhouette of a house and heard some noise. Grabbing my arm, Tashi caught me out of the darkness and led me to a wall bordering the stream, which somehow Sonam had scrambled up. I felt some sharp pains in my chest as he pulled me up the side of a terrace banked with thorny bushes. I was too frightened to back down and continued to scramble on to what seemed to be a terraced field.

I winched as more thorns gored my chest. In the field it was much lighter, and I had just made out a house to our right when I heard a man's voice. My heart pounded. I began to run blindly behind my companions and fell headlong over the edge of a terrace on to a lower field. Frantically I picked myself up to follow the others who were climbing over the loose stones of a wall that they had brought down with a crash. We were now in a narrow, walled-in path. Behind us voices were coming from the house. Had we been spotted in the field? Could that have been the police post? My heart sank, but Tashi and Sonam urged me on and crouching down we continued between the two walls, not away from the house but towards it again. On tiptoe we passed against its wall. I heard voices. Surely we would be caught. I realized that we were now in the middle of a village, travelling between more houses, but the voices had stopped. We rushed on as quietly as we could, and once more came upon the stream with its mud slurp obliterating the trail.

Twenty minutes later Sonam and Tashi stopped. We were clear, they said, and should rest for a little while. My heart still thumping, I went to the stream in the dark and filled my mug with water which I drank, shivering in the cold. Sonam produced some apricots and a chapati, and we sat munching in silence. I looked at my watch; it was ten-thirty. We had been on the trail for three and a half hours and, except for the dismal wait by the stream near Lotsum, I had been walking since midday. This whole affair was taking on the aspect of a nightmare. The constant darkness had begun to give me claustrophobia, and I felt as if we had been walking in circles. When and where were we going to sleep? Could we afford to stop and sleep here so close to Tatsa? Sonam and Tashi did not answer me but soon got up. We were carrying on.

The landscape began slowly to change, or so it seemed, the river becoming once again hemmed in by cliffs. Up rose the path along a narrow ledge; one step misplaced and I would break my neck. In several places the flash flood had brought down the trail that hung to the sides of the canyon. Frequently we came upon gaping voids which forced us to scale down the cliffs in the dark back to the river and wander along its banks until we found the trail once more. Again and again landslides compelled us to repeat the manoeuvre. More and more often Sonam used the torch. I was afraid this would give us away, but the trail on its ledge, with these breaks, was far too dangerous to follow in the dark.

It would be boring to recount in detail the sweat and anguish that dogged me during the next three hours as we continued to climb ever up, heading for the village of Karet. Finally it was announced with a fright as something, it must have been a yak, moved by our side. I could not see the lie of the land but noticed a light twinkling on the other side of the valley. We came upon a lone dwelling, passing under its wall in silence. The occupants were probably asleep. To my relief no dogs barked. We then ran into a herd of horses that stampeded with much noise, frightening me yet again. It was two o'clock in the morning when, after having climbed a steep slope strewn with rocks that jingled beneath our feet, Sonam and Tashi announced that we were stopping to sleep. I was in a daze, totally exhausted. I lay down where I stood, resting my head on my damp hat. Only then did I notice that it was snowing: a light snow that pattered on my shawl that I was using as a blanket. At first, listening to the breathing of my companions, between whom I lay, I could not sleep. Then, mercifully, in spite of the cold, I passed out into a heavy slumber.

All too soon I was awoken by Sonam calling my name. 'What time is it?' I asked, looking for my watch on my wrist. It was not there. Then I remembered that it was hidden in my pocket. It was three o'clock in the morning; we had slept but an hour. What was the matter, I recall thinking, but there was no answer, for the men had once again begun to climb. There was now no semblance of a trail. We advanced over huge slabs of stone, following a dark rivulet that ran to our left. It was still snowing little crystals of ice. The sky was dark, and again and again I tripped, thanking God I had brought my rugged pair of shoes; never would I have made it in the gym shoes I had bought in Kargil.

The air was bitterly cold and I began to feel the familiar effects of high altitude. We were rising fast, heading towards that elusive pass whose name constantly echoed in my mind – Shashi-la, the pass that would lead us up to the watershed. I was now deep inside the forbidden triangle, out in the open, plodding ever up what seemed like steps of loose rock. It was four-thirty or five, I do not remember exactly, when the men halted again beside a tiny trickle of water. Here grew a small solitary willow, whose branches we snapped to make a fire. This was, I understood, the last water on our route. They were making tea. It had stopped snowing, but I was now seized with violent fits of shivering that the tiny fire could not control. From the pocket of my mountain trousers, hidden under my baggy pants, I pulled out my 'space blanket'. I had brought it along thinking of some kind of emergency. I now wrapped it around me and found that it warmed my body slightly as I sat nose into the smoke of the fire.

Against the flames I saw the faces of my two friends: the mobile features of Sonam, like some scrawny shepherd from Greece, and Tashi, thin and emaciated. To me they both seemed out of place, ill adapted to such terrain, too European to fit here into the rugged Himalayan landscape. Although I had witnessed their energy, their skill on the trail, it was hard to accept that here, unlike me, they were at home. This was their territory, and not, as I had so long believed, that of Tibetan-speaking Mongolian people. Here were men who retained a faith that was similar to that of neolithic men, who believed that their dead should be buried with food and possessions for a journey to the Land of the Fairies. This was a world in which water and fire played sacred roles, for they are indeed what make survival possible, as we experienced at this last halting place before the arid, waterless expanse of the great ridges.

All too soon we again took to the road.

'Where shall we sleep?' I asked, worried.

'On the other side,' Tashi said, 'in our *brok* above Dartzig.' A *brok* is a high altitude pasture.

It was still dark as we set off, but soon the pale glow of dawn announced a sinister, cloudy day. We were now walking up the cascading steps of the little dry rivulet by which we had made the fire. As light slowly parted the darkness I could see that we were climbing a causeway of great slabs hemmed into a gully, with here and there a pool of water that disappeared into the rocks. On several occasions the gully forked, but we clung to the right branch and soon I could see above me a desolate stony ridge. This I mistook for the pass, but Tashi said it was still another hour or two to the summit. By now I was completely exhausted, and the altitude made me puff like an ox. Nothing seemed to slow the pace of my friends, however, whom I now begged to stop every once in a while so that I could catch my breath. Would I make it? I began to worry, seeing that the ridge above me revealed yet another, even higher and more desolate. Looking back all I could see were barren slopes, with no sight of where we had passed during the night, that long night that seemed like a black dream. My heart raced, and the blood beat at my temples. Every ten minutes I asked if we were nearing the top. It was eight o'clock in the morning; I had been walking, in the dark, for twelve hours, not counting the one hour's sleep out in the open.

Finally there appeared a remote ridge that definitely seemed to be the last, although there was no *chorten* or monument to mark a pass. Summoning all my energy I clambered up the last gradient. It was snowing again, and this time the flakes were larger. My heart beat ever faster when at last I joined my companions on the summit, yelling at them quickly to go down a few yards so as not to be seen on the crest.

At long last I had reached my goal. I now stood, at 17,000 feet, in the centre of the strategic triangle from which I had been banned, in the heart of Minaro territory. From the vantage point of the pass I could at last examine the Land of the Dards. The journey which I had thought would take two days, we had accomplished in a twelve-hour marathon – a route of anxiety and weariness for which I was now well rewarded. Beneath me lay the staggering landscape of the Minaro's forbidden fold, the answer to the enigma of Minaro survival.

Snow was still falling, yet through it I could see the amazing panorama. Everywhere before me the landscape tumbled towards the Indus. At first it fell in great swooping shale-covered ridges which to the north rolled down to a lower crest, upon which five *chortens* marked the trail that led to Dartzig. Across to my right was the Shahi-tang, a high barren plain barred by a great stone wall that had once dammed what little water there was to collect here. Most stunning was the view to the west, a succession of ridges that fell to the junction of the Suru and the Indus, behind which rose tier upon tier of barren ranges to the far distant horizon.

By any reckoning it was a barren landscape, but one I now knew to conceal an immense wealth, for here was the land of the ibex, the abode of fairies that guarded the flocks of the goddess of fortune. Here also lived the goddess of fertility who oversaw the destiny of the people of Dartzig and Garkund, of Hanu and Dah. And there, far to my left, I could make out the Dansar Plain, the land of the gold-digging 'ants' – the land of legend, inaccessible El Dorado of the Greeks, the lost horizon that so many people had sought from as far away as Greece and the Sea of China, from Mongolia to India, and which no one had yet found. '*Fertilissimi sunt auri Dardae.*' Yes, how rich; but it was not for wealth that I had come, taking such foolish risks, but for the joy of laying my eyes upon this forbidden landscape.

My reward was to have witnessed the past and to have experienced the bonds of friendship which united me with my companions. I had also acquired a treasury of information regarding our early history. I now had a clear insight into the obscure world of our ancient ancestors – a world hitherto known only through the mute tokens of lost stone axes, or the silent messages to be read in long abandoned graves. At last, for me, our ancestors had faces. The men who had huddled in caves I now saw as Sonam and Tashi, little different from ourselves in either appearance, hopes or feelings. Like us, caught between birth and death, they queried the heavens for answers to the enigma of man's existence. They believed, I now knew, in a goddess, the mother of nature, creator of all living beings and provider of all goodness, attended by a legion of fairies dwelling on hill tops, near springs and in trees. Men turned to her in hope, gratitude and despair. There was nothing fearful in their beliefs, nothing awe-inspiring about their goddesses who regulated the seasons, directed their arrows and blessed them with children. Like nature itself, their divinities were neither deliberately cruel nor benevolent but ruled as messengers of eternal hope.

I now better understood how our own spiritual beliefs had evolved over the ages: how the rule of women had in time led to the rule of men, benevolent Mother Nature giving way to Babalachen, the Father God, earthly kings arising to rule in his name. How the advent of stable agriculture had led to the exploitation of man by man, their arrows directed away from the hunt to the business of war. Later, surrounded by neolithic herders, the first tyrants arose – Darius, Alexander – claiming to be agents of the gods. The greater the force, the greater the divinity; the more powerful the tyrant, the more fearful his gods. Babalachen, the Great Father, became the

Tibetan god of war. The evolution of monotheism led rulers to declare the superiority of their particular divinity. In this certainty the Chinese ordained their emperors the Sons of God, the Christians crowned their kings with divine right, and later Moslem rulers swept across the globe imposing their mandate from heaven with drawn swords. As a result, there were few in Europe or Asia who escaped conquest or conversion. The Minaro were among the very last to survive, locked away in their stronghold which was now spread out before me: the last, inaccessible bowels of the earth, the most remote corner of the world's most rugged terrain.

Now I knew how similar people had once populated all of Europe and most of Asia, leaving here a carved ibex, there a standing stone: mementos of gratitude or signposts of the seasons, expressions of their love and respect for nature and mankind. Here in the very heart of the Himalayas, beyond the grasp of the Tibetan Empire, the Greeks, the Chinese and the Pan-Islamic powers, had survived the last denizens of what was, all told, a better world.

How long would the Minaro be able to survive? Were there not cannon trained on their villages from either side of the cease-fire line, at the order of zealous, intolerant, modern empires? India claiming the area as her legacy from the British, Pakistan ruling in strictest accordance with the laws of Mohammed, anxious to convert the last infidels of Little Tibet? The hour, alas, had come when the fairies must die.

I felt sad for what I knew must soon be the end of the world of the Minaro. I asked myself how much I had really learnt, as I contemplated the long trail that began at Harvard when, as a young man, I crossed the bridge to the Peabody Museum, curious to discover more about our ancestors, a trail I could see stretching far out over the Himalayas of Nepal to the gullies of Mustang, clambering up the forest-clad ridges of Bhutan, meandering through the western Himalayan deserts to lead, at last, to this lonely ridge. Had I been chasing an imaginary El Dorado – not that of the ants, but the dream of a lost paradise? What, in truth, had I achieved other than satisfying my curiosity as to who had drawn the bison which so fascinated me as a child. Did the Stone Age really hold an answer to the anxieties that assail mankind? Did my companions have a reply to the eternal questions of why we are born and why we must die?

Whom to believe, the fairy goddesses, or the one God Almighty? Was life a mere struggle to come to terms with death or, as the Buddhists claim, to discover that it is all meaningless? Do the long, arduous trails of life lead to nothing beyond the fleeting instant we call the present – obscured as it is by dreams of the future, haunted by visions of the past? Or perhaps, as the Minaro believed, the answer was unrelated to either the past or the future, relying on simple, daily contact with nature itself.

The snowstorm was lashing around us, blotting out the landscape as the wind ran up the Indus, the wind that had scattered the story of this land's wealth far beyond the enclosing passes that forbade its access.

Rapt as I was in the scene before me, I could not forget the dangers of the moment. Standing out in the open, in daylight, we could easily be spotted by passing patrols. Somewhere beneath ran the cease-fire line, the central focus of man's hatred. I was now deep within forbidden territory, exhausted by more than fifty miles of nearly continuous walking and climbing since I had left Missy in Sershing. I had slept but one hour in all that time.

Crossing over the pass, we began to make for the ridge leading to the cattle shelter of the Dartzig people. As we plodded towards the Indus the snow began to fall thicker than before, clinging to the frozen ground. I had planned for nearly every occurrence but this. Tashi and I began to argue. If we carried on and slept in the cattle shelter, he claimed, the snow might block the pass and cut off our retreat. It would be too dangerous to weather the storm in the cattle shelter, for there was no telling how long we might be trapped there, or who might come along.

By now we had descended the ridge from the pass leading to the *chortens* that, partially veiled by snow, ghosted with their silhouettes the place where the trail fell vertically down towards Dartzig. What should we do? Rigid with exhaustion, cold and anxiety, fearing the worst from the snowstorm, I decided that we had come far enough. We could not risk being trapped within the inner line, beyond the pass. The time had come for me to turn back. Huddling together we made it back up the ridge to the Shashi-la. My hands numb with cold, I searched for a stone and then saw what I was looking for, a slab of rock just off the pass. I knelt down and began, in the now familiar manner of our neolithic ancestors, to peck at the rock, carving my initials, a reminder of my passage. An arrogant and perhaps stupid gesture to testify that I had, at long last, from this spot contemplated the land that all had believed to be a myth.

Having thus left my mark I struggled on in the windswept snow along the ridge that joined the Shashi-la with the lower Bu-la. Now we had to face new problems. There was no question of returning in daylight by the route up which we had come. We had therefore decided to travel back high up beneath the base of the mountain that, to the west, separated the valley of Lotsum from Kargil. We planned to follow, we hoped unseen, the foot of the cliffs that rose to its summit, turning round the mountain until we were above the lower part of the valley of Lotsum. We would then stop and sleep, awaiting nightfall before descending a gully that we believed would lead us down to the Lotsum valley below Tatsa.

After half an hour we reached the Bu-la pass; here we found a trench dug out on the very summit, a machine-gun post. This reminder of the military made me shudder. The snow had now eased up a little and from the Bu-la I could clearly see below us the strategic road leading down from the Hambuting-la to the Indus, passing the Minaro hamlets of Lalung and Tsilmo before it turned out of sight towards Dartzig. I now had a clearer view of where the Suru and Shingo rivers joined the Indus just below the ceasefire line. Beyond the Indus I could clearly see Dapsar, the plain of the gold-digging marmots.

Realizing that if we could see the road and the villages we could also be seen, I reluctantly turned my back on the land of the Minaro, no doubt for ever. We descended from the Bu-la, taking a traverse towards the great mountain. In the shelter of a gully we stopped. It was ten-thirty and still snowing; I lay down and fell asleep for a while as the men tried to make a fire. Less than an hour later we began our long and dangerous retreat, in view of Karet, whose surprisingly dark houses of adobe lay clustered below us.

It was nearly three-thirty when at last we camped in a narrow canyon that we hoped would lead us down to the valley below Tatsa. There was no telling where we were in relation to the village, concealed in its gorge. Now began again a long wait for nightfall during which, in fear of being discovered, I slept only occasionally.

It was 7 p.m. and dark when we struck out down the gully until we hit the trail of the night before. We were uncertain as to exactly where we had joined it, and could not tell if Tatsa was above or below us. Alas we had come down too high and soon ran into the village which, to my surprise, was full of people still threshing the harvest upon the very terraces over which we had fallen the night before. It had stopped snowing and the night was clear. In Tatsa we bumped into a crowd of men and women, some of whom began to march down the trail with us. One woman brushed against me and started to talk. Clinging to my sack with my hands concealing my face, slouched in my best Minaro gait, I pretended not to hear. Hurrying on I slipped down the trail, Sonam and Tashi hard on my heels. It had been a close shave.

Three hours later, at about ten-thirty, we reached Lotsum after having lost our way in the river near the village. Suddenly we found ourselves surrounded by houses. In an instant I pulled the cord of my baggy pants, and they fell to the ground. Hastily I tucked my shirt into my trousers, Tashi packed my shawl and my hat in his bag, and then, as if nothing had happened, I found myself once again in Western guise upon the metalled road. We had made it. I was safe at last.

In a little under thirty-four hours I had walked approximately sixty-eight miles, most of them within the inner line of India's most strategically important frontier.

Once back on the road we were at a loss what to do. There were no lights in the bazaar so we wandered up the highway for a while until we saw the lights of a truck coming towards us. Should I stop it? What if it were a military vehicle? I now noticed that it had a blue light. It must be a police jeep or an army truck. Caught in the headlights, just before being dazzled, I noticed that it was a civilian vehicle. It came to a halt with a screech of tyres and we hitched a ride.

An hour later, on entering Kargil, the truck was stopped and searched by an officer of the Border Security Force, no doubt wondering what it was doing so late at night on the military highway. We smiled as he waved us on into the darkened bazaar. I made for the first hotel and ordered several bottles of Indian beer, which the three of us drank before happily falling into a dead sleep.

The following morning I secured a jeep and we set off to join Missy at Sershing, passing Lotsum, a village whose name I would never forget. Having reached Shergol, we sped up the half washed-away trail to within three hundred yards of Sershing. I ran over to the camp and there, to my amazement, standing before our tent, was Nordrop. My wife rushed out to greet us, explaining how Nordrop had arrived the very evening after our departure from Kargil. Directed by Mr Kakpori he had found our camp with some difficulty. Of all the messages we had sent he had received only the last given to a German tourist.

After exchanging news and taking some photographs of me in disguise, we drove back to Kargil all together, in the highest of spirits.

POSTSCRIPT

The time had come for us to leave India and finally appraise what we had accomplished in the four years we had devoted to studying the Minaro.

With us we now brought back the largest vocabulary to date of the Minaro's archaic Indo-European language, along with a vast store of information on their social and religious beliefs – a detailed record of rites and rituals of which only a synopsis, perforce, has found its way into this book.

This information has allowed us to establish beyond doubt that the Minaro are the last heirs to both ancient Aryan and pre-Aryan traditions, voices from a past believed to have been muted for ever. If yet much work remains to be done, we believe we have established a firm basis for further studies.

We also derived great satisfaction in having identified the lost Minaro colonies of Zanskar, and in having established the unquestionable link between Minaro beliefs and Tibet's little known 'religion of men', a link which opens new perspectives for the study of the earliest creeds of Central Asia.

As for our last journey, in which we had sacrificed prudence for passion, it had not been in vain. My brief glimpse at the forbidden land well rewarded years of frustration, while in the process of getting there we had not only come to a better understanding of the Minaro's world, but had also, in the end, solved the 2,500 year mystery of the ants' gold. Any ire our actions may cause will, we hope, only help attract attention to the urgency for government-assisted, scientific expeditions to the area.

I hope that our mission, if desperate, was not in vain. Herodotus had now been vindicated; the land of the gold-digging ants, or rather marmots, truly exists. It lies in the plain of Dansar, two miles east of Morol, a mile and a half west of Ganosh, latitude 34° 46′ North, longitude 76° 15′ East.

I leave its gold for others to collect.

Cadaques 1984.

INDEX

Abdullah, Sheikh, 'Lion of Kashmir', 13–15; 64, 66–7; 81, 110, 112–3, 123; death of, 126–7
Abi-lamo (or Mu-shiring-men), goddess, 42, 44
Abilhamo (goddess of fertility), 48
Afghanistan, 11, 124
Alchi monastery, 72
Alexander the Great, 2–3, 11, 30, 79, 89, 96, 108; Indian campaign of, 116–8
Allen, 'Missy', 10, 22, 31, 46, 64–5, 111, 129, 132–3, 154–5, 175; meeting with, 4–5; as village nurse, 24–5; knee problem of, 36, 52, 67, 107, 139–42
Almeido, Diego d', 20
Arderkaro, the, see Drok-pa
Aryans and Aryanism, 3, 8–9, 22, 49, 68, 72, 86, 88, 90, 94, 114, 146–7, 175
Ashoka, King, 12, 81
Aspasians, the, see Gureans
Assacenians, the, see Gureans

Babalachen, 'Father God': cult of, 42, 44–5, 47–8, 85, 88, 92, 170
Bacartse (Minaro village), 44
Ba-lu Khar fortress, 81–2
Balti, the, 119
Basardik stone, 98
Basenden (fairy goddess of pastures), 136
Batalik (Minaro town), 125

Buddhism, 20, 28–9, 68, 106, 138; its tolerance of other beliefs, 30, 32, 53–4, 136; introduced into Tibet 152–3
Bhutan, 27, 32, 37, 99, 115, 157, 162
Bonono festival, 68–9
Bon priests, 92
Boston, 2, 63
Burns, Prof. A. R., 146

Chemet (elder of Khalatse village), 80
China, 11–12, 17, 20, 45; Great Wall of, 100, 108–9; invades Mongolia, 108
Chrysostom, Dio, 2
Clark, Graham E., 7, 89

Dah (Minaro village), 41, 55, 59, 60, 78, 93
Dal Lake, 11, 15
Dansar, plain of, 170, 173, 176; gold collecting in, 144–8
Dardistan, 6–7
Dards, the (or Dardicae, Darade), 2, 4, 7, 9, 17, 35, 50, 59, 63, 94, 145, · 147–8; see also Drok-pa and Minaro
Dartzig (Minaro village), 55, 59–60, 125, 128–9; festivals of, 136, 144; gold collecting in, 144–5, 148
David-Neel, Alexandra, 111
Delhi, New, 10, 12, 64–5
Deosai plateau, 119–20
Deseredi, 20

177

Do-ring, standing stones at, 32
Dras river, 17
Dras (village), 17, 68, 124
Drok-pa, the (or Arderkaro, Dards),
 3–5, 7, 9, 34–5, 45, 72, 108, 138;
 see also Minaro; Dards

Farouq (son of Sheikh Abdullah), 127
Francke, Rev. A. K., 7–9, 35, 59,
 69–70, 74–5, 81, 138, 146–7
Fussman, G., 94

Gandhi, Mrs Indira, 64–7, 110, 112
Ganges river, 63–4
Garkund (Minaro village), 41, 55,
 59–60, 69, 125
Gergan, S. S., 75
Gilgit, 8–9, 13, 20, 59, 60, 69, 89, 94
Gureans, the (or Assacenians,
 Aspasians), 117, 123
Gyagam (Minaro village), 35–7,
 44–5, 88, 90, 91–3, 95–100; New
 Year celebrations in, 40; religion
 in, 42; fortress of, 50, 55
Gyalpo Pong Kham (Drok-pa chief),
 legend of, 40
Gyantse-Lhamo (fairy goddess of
 fortune), 85, 87, 88, 91–3, 139, 153

Hameling (Minaro village), 34, 40,
 44, 45; religion in, 42; fortress of,
 50, 55
Hanu (Minaro village), 34, 40–41, 55
Harvard University, 3, 4, 66; Business
 School, 2, 4
Herodotus, 1–2, 4–5, 7–8, 15, 61–3,
 74–5, 82, 85, 104, 145–8, 176
Herrmann, Prof. A., 6, 73–5, 146–7
Himalayas, the, 1, 7, 9, 11–12, 16,
 19–20, 24, 27, 30, 33, 42, 80, 91,
 103, 107, 157, 162
Hitler, Adolf, 3, 8
Hiung-nu, the (early Mongolians),
 108–9
Hunza kingdom, 121

ibex, 45–7; appearance and habitat of,
 101
ibex carvings, 26–30, 33–4, 40–2,
 46–9, 69–70, 72, 81, 87, 98, 100,
 119–20, 152
India, 1, 10–11, 17, 20, 56, 63, 94,
 110, 114, 121, 122, 124, 171, 174;
 bureaucracy in 12–14, 16, 64–6,
 112, 150; Alexander's campaign in,
 116–8
Indus river, 3, 6, 8, 12, 20, 55, 59,
 61, 72, 83, 84, 118, 125, 173; gold
 in, 73, 75
Islam, 16, 20, 30, 94, 120
Islamabad, 116

Jettmar, Prof. Karl, 94, 120

Kadakh, 15
Kailash, the, 42, 90, 117; resemblance
 to the Minaro, 121
Kakpori, Ghulam Muhammed, 18,
 55, 58, 68–9, 91, 126, 132, 175
Kanishka, King, 28, 53, 139
Karakoram range, 11, 13, 112, 118
Kargil, 14–15, 17, 20, 124, 128
Karmay, Samten, 138n
Karsha monastery, 29, 100–1
Kartsé (Minaro village), 55, 134,
 137–8; giant Buddha of, 137–9
Kashmir, 3, 10, 11, 13, 15, 20; visit
 of Dalai Lama to, 53–55; see also
 Abdullah, Sheikh
Khalatse, 20, 73–4, 77–82
Konchet, cleft rock at, 33
Koros, Csomo de, 103, 111
Kushu-lo-Lhamo (goddess of
 weather), 85

Ladakh, 3, 6, 7–8, 10, 12, 14, 15, 20,
 53; tourism in, 18; goldfields of,
 66–7, 75; monasteries of, 72;
 polyandry in, 84; as military
 stronghold, 124; visit of Dalai
 Lama to, 53–5, 152–3

Lamaism, Tibetan, 54–5, 71–2, 83
Lamayuru monastery, 55, 82–3
Laufer, B., 5, 147
Leh, capital of Ladakh, 7, 14–5, 20,
    70–1
Leitner, G. W., 6–7, 8, 17, 25
Lepcha country, 27, 33
Lhasa, capital of Tibet, 17, 20, 83
'lightning stones', 27, 33, 49
Lingshit monastery, 83
Lorimer, Lt. Col. D. L. R., 94
Lotsum (village), 1, 128, 151, 158,
    161–2, 174

Mahomed, Ghulam, 8
Marco Polo, 19–20
Marutse (Minaro village), 44
Marx, Rev. Karl, 7–8
Megasthenes, 2, 75, 148
Minaro, the, 9–10, 12, 17; villages of,
    34–7; language of, 40, 60, 78, 117;
    dress of, 41–2, 61, 68, 84, 88;
    pagan traditions of, 42–5; religious
    freedom of, 44; hatred of the cow,
    45; hunting customs of, 43–6, 59;
    origins of, 46, 49–50; of the Indus
    valley, 55–62, 77–80, 82–90;
    polyandry among, 84–5;
    matriarchal society of, 85; religion
    and rituals of, 85–8, 92–4, 96, 98,
    136; social system of, 95–6; burial
    customs of, 97; ancient way of life
    of, 105–6; women, 62, 80, 84–5; see
    also Drok-pa
Mongolians, the, 22, 26, 35, 39, 135, 168
Moorcroft, William, 21, 103, 147
Mulbekh, 3, 7, 83–4, 139, 143, 158
Mu-shiring-men, Queen of Fairies,
    see Abi-lamo
Mustang, 32, 52, 65, 83

Na luk (Minaro warlord), 77–8
Namgyal, Dorje (Minaro of
    Garkund), 58–62, 84–6

Nanak, Guru, 15
Nearchos, 75, 145
Nordrop, Lama, 15, 21, 28, 29, 69,
    71, 91, 94, 100, 104, 106–7, 123,
    175; appearance of, 22–3;
    relationship with author, 24; piety
    of, 38; as interpreter, 39, 60
Nysa (ancient town of Indus valley),
    116–7

Pakistan, 1, 8–9, 12–13, 26, 42, 69,
    110, 114, 116, 118, 121–2, 124, 171
Pang-gong salt lake, 32
Peabody Museum, 4, 171
Pensi-la pass, 34, 91, 98
Persians, the, 89, 116, 145, 147
Petech, Prof. Luciano, 8, 33, 81
Phokar Dzong shrine, 152–4
Pliny the Elder, 2

Rangdum monastery, 23, 44, 83, 99
'religion of men', 33–4, 41–2, 53,
    91–2, 175
Remala (Minaro village), 35–6, 40;
    religion in, 42
Rimpoche, Guru, 152–3
Ritter, C., 6, 147
Roerich, George N., 31–2, 68, 92
Rolagong valley, 23, 51–2
Rongdu, 55
Rupchu plains, 35, 90–1, 100, 105
Rusi-la pass, 128, 139
Rindzing, Tsewan (Minaro priest),
    47–9, 91, 94–5, 98

Sani monastery, 31
Sapi-chu river, 141–2
Sapi-la pass, 128, 139, 143
Scythians, the, 31, 43, 61, 87–8, 89,
    90, 97, 109
Sershing village, 143, 159, 175
Shahi-tang plain, 169
Shadi village, 108–9
Shashi-la pass, 151, 162, 172

Shaw, R. B., 8, 25, 60
Shi Hwang-ti (1st Emperor of
    China), 108
Shins, the, 8–9, 17, 94, 118, 120–1
Shiringmen-Lhamo (fairy goddess of
    fertility), 85, 93, 153
Sikkim, 27
Silk Route, the, 20
Skardo, capital of Baltistan, 13, 20,
    89, 118–9
Sonam (author's Minaro porter),
    author's journey with, 129–74
Songtsen Gampo (King of Tibet), 71
Srinagar, capital of Kashmir, 10, 11,
    15, 122
standing stones, 31–2, 68, 93, 100
Stein, Sir Aurel, 5
Stirajya, 'Eastern Kingdom of
    Women' (or Suvarnagotra, 'Race of
    Gold'), 62
Strabo, 2, 75
Suru valley, 6, 55, 134
Sutledge river, 6
Suvarnagotra, see Stirajya

Tarn, W. W., 117
Tashi (author's Minaro porter),
    author's journey with, 129–74
Thunri (village), 25–6, 34–5
Tibet, 2, 3, 9, 11, 16–17, 20, 22,
    26–7, 45, 46, 54, 69, 70; creation of,
28; ancient cults of, 30–4, 37;
    Kingdom established, 71; struggle
    with Minaro, 78; Minaro chased
    from, 90; polyandry in, 84;
    'religion of men' in, 91–2;
    individualism in, 95–6; Buddhism
    introduced to, 152–3; see also
    Lamaism
Tikse monastery, 71
Tucci, Prof. Giuseppe, 8, 26, 34

Ubima Kavthisa (Kushan king), 81
Umasi-la pass, 24

Waka river, 157
Weidner Library, 4–5, 8

Yellow river, 5

Zangla, King of, 102–3
Zangla region, 102–3
Zangmanden-Lhamo (protective
    goddess of village and hunters), 85
Zail Singh, 66–7, 110
Zanskar (region of Ladakh), 14, 15,
    24, 38, 41, 44–5, 50; standing
    stones and ibex drawings at, 32;
    funeral rites in, 32–3; visit of Dalai
    Lama to, 53–5; gold panning in,
    73; polyandry in, 84
Zoji-la pass, 16, 65, 68, 124